DISCOVER
BEDFORDSHIRE'S
PAST

Dennis Bidwell

COUNTRYSIDE BOOKS
NEWBURY, BERKSHIRE

C000117506

COUNTRYSIDE BOOKS
3 Catherine Road
Newbury, Berkshire

To view our complete range of books,
please visit us at
www.countrysidebooks.co.uk

ISBN 1 85306 705 9

The front cover photograph of the ruins of Houghton House
and the back cover photograph of the statue of John Bunyan
both taken by the author

Designed by Graham Whiteman

Produced through MRM Associates Ltd., Reading
Printed in England by J.W. Arrowsmith Ltd., Bristol

FOREWORD

The chance to produce something quite different from a guide book or history book was what appealed to me about writing this book. In wondering what form it should take, I remembered when I peddled my bike across the county, half a century ago, and gleaned stories from folks only too pleased to talk about their community – and keep a young lad enthralled.

Retracing those youthful steps, this time by car, has helped me put together a selection of Bedfordshire titbits ranging from Harrold, where they built their lock-up round so that the devil would have no corner to hide in, to Flitton where curative powers were thought to emanate from the spot where a highwayman was shot and buried.

Many changes have occurred across Bedfordshire. Villages like Flitwick have expanded into towns but others have remained small enough to be just part of a parish. Old cottages have been transformed into desirable residences, so have some of our beautiful tithe barns, like Felmersham's for instance.

For many years, Bernard B. West, RIBA, faithfully recorded our county's changing scenes in his finely detailed sketches and popular water-colours. His regular contributions to that mine of county knowledge the previously published 'Bedfordshire Magazine' were entitled *Sketch-Book* and permission to use these illustrations is gratefully acknowledged. Some scenes show little change, others reveal interesting differences through the march of time, perhaps with a hint of nostalgia.

Acknowledgements are extended to the Library Service, together with the Public Record Office and the many contributors to those local interest sections so conscientiously maintained. Special thanks go to my wife Betty who typed every single word and remained supportive throughout.

Dennis Bidwell

AMPTHILL

This well-known Georgian market town nestles in the centre of the county, slowing traffic at its crossroads and giving motorists time to wonder at its 'olde worlde' charm. The picturesque Market Square dates from the 1780s and through archways and alleyways peep buildings from the 17th century, some with pargeting which displays the fleur-de-lis.

There is something of interest in every direction from the tiny gazebo in Dunstable Street which 'old wives tales' tell us was where Catherine of Aragon taught the town lace-making to Church Street and a superb Jacobean house where Edmund Wingate lived, a clever mathematician who gave the world the slide rule and taught Henrietta Maria, wife of Charles I to speak English.

On the opposite side of the road stand exquisite iron gates barely glanced at by residents but enough to hold the attention of a discerning stranger. They are from the early 18th century and their quality has been acknowledged by naming the residence 'Gates House'.

So easily missed, yet overlooking Ampthill, stands Houghton House, now in ruins, that was 'House Beautiful' in John Bunyan's *The Pilgrim's Progress*. It was built by Mary Herbert, Dowager Countess of Pembroke, from a design thought to be Italian. It was a most unusual structure at the time, being compact and elegant, with pinnacles at each corner tower and plenty of bay windows. This was Mary's dream house and she settled down there, amongst literary friends of the day, to prepare her late brother's work for publication. He was Sir Philip Sidney, a favourite of Queen Elizabeth I who gave him a state funeral.

At long last a royal visit was made to Ampthill and King James I stayed at Houghton House in 1621, putting the stamp of approval on Mary's creation. Shortly afterwards the popular Countess died and the house took on a chequered existence until, in 1738, it was acquired by the Duke of Bedford, the largest landowner in the county.

In due course, his heir, Francis the young Marquis of Tavistock, moved in with his beautiful wife Elizabeth, daughter of the Earl of Albermarle, and they soon had a young family. It was a happy time but then Francis was thrown from his horse and badly injured. He died waiting for a doctor to arrive from London, even though a local doctor could have saved his life. Elizabeth could not be consoled and died shortly afterwards.

Perhaps because of all the sadness the death knell had already been sounded for 'House Beautiful' and in 1794 the Duke ordered the house to be stripped of everything valuable and de-roofed to let the elements do their worst.

ARLESEY

One of the longest villages around – it stretches for over three miles down the valley of the river Hiz, alongside the main London to Scotland railway line and it was on this stretch of track that the rail disaster of 1876 occurred, two days before Christmas.

Events that culminated in the crash started when the 2.45pm GNR express left Kings Cross heading north non-stop to Peterborough. Bad weather and some snow on the lines made the going hard to start with but, nearing Arlesey, the situation improved so the driver increased speed to nearly 70 miles per hour, to make up for lost time.

What the driver didn't know was that a goods train heading for London on the down line had been allowed to cross the main line to pick up more waggons in a siding. The signal man knew about the express heading their way but there was plenty of time for the manoeuvre so he switched it through. The engine was pulling 25 waggons and they all got across until the 22nd one and that came off the rails, followed by the last two and the guard's van.

Frantically men rushed to the scene in a vain attempt to clear the line but one waggon alone had a nine ton load and there was no shifting it. They were helpless to stop the express; the driver saw the bright lights ahead and the red stop signal but the brakes were ineffective on the slippery rails. The impact was horrendous: the engine rose over one of the waggons, detaching itself from the tender, and the six front carriages piled up into the wreckage.

The driver, fireman and four passengers died. Thirty people were injured and horses were quickly saddled to get word to Biggleswade that doctors were needed. It was a bad day all round but the railways were expanding and fortunately accidents were fairly rare.

It was the railways which brought prosperity to Arlesey in the 19th century when industry came, like Roger Beart's brickworks which had their own main line link. Although the works are closed now, since the clay ran out, the lovely yellow brick houses in the area serve as a permanent reminder.

ASPLEY GUISE

—— Once described as an aristocratic village, Aspley Guise enjoys its favoured location amongst pine trees and sand hills next door to Woburn. In 1845 *The Gentleman's Magazine* reported that it was well known for the number of genteel families it contained.

The moated farmstead of Bury Farm, Astwick

In 1849 Dr Williams, a surgeon, took over a local practice. He was impressed by the Aspley Heath area but concerned that it had 'fallen into the hands of a distinct colony of independent settlers'.

He was not the only one to have been concerned about the erection of cottages on parish land. It was feared this would be followed by claims for freehold rights. In one notable incident in 1833, ten angry men met at the Bell public house to discuss the cottage of one John Rudkin on the Heath, then they marched over and demolished it.

A quarrel, long past, between two of the gentry was blamed for originally diverting attention from the Heath. The protagonists were embroiled for 14 years. One was Richard How, of elegant Aspley House, a Quaker and major landowner. The other was Francis Moore, a young man from the West Country trying to make his way in the world. The issue was the setting of a poor rate in 1770 over which the young man had taken the initiative, apparently rather rashly as he had overcharged Richard How and his tenants. They appealed to have the figure rejected and won the day, but animosity reigned from then on.

Aspley Guise is a flourishing village and has come a long way since the de Guise family, from whom it got its name, swapped it with Henry VIII in 1540 for land in Gloucestershire.

ASTWICK

——— This is a tiny place close to Stotfold and the A1 which marks the county boundary at this point. Astwick means 'good pasture in the east'. It was a farming community and the site was known to the Romans, building their Great North Road.

The Beauchamps of Bedford held Astwick after 1066 but they sub-let to a man called Bernard who then assumed the name de Astwick. By 1679 there were two manors, and a small manor house, held by William de Astwick.

The church would have been fairly new then and destined to become the only church in the county dedicated to St Guthlac of Lincolnshire. Guthlac was a wild young man, belonging to the Mercian royal family of the 7th century, and spent many youthful years involved in warfare. Later, perhaps because of his battle experiences, he joined the monastic community at Repton. Many years later he built a cell on the Isle of Crowland in the fens and became a hermit renowned for his love of birds. People would travel miles for his spiritual guidance and when he died in 714 King Ethelbald built a great Benedictine Abbey in his memory.

BARTON-LE-CLAY

——— Thanks to a bypass, Barton-le-Clay has regained its main street, but it is now all too easy to travel between Bedford and Luton with hardly a glimpse of this large village at the end of the Chilterns.

Things were very different in the days before 1832 – when a cutting was made – as the rolling Barton Hills to the south of the village had to be negotiated by coach and horses, and accidents were common. In 1665 a traveller on his way to Houghton Conquest was pitched out of his coach-top seat by the steep descent into the village and landed on the road. Unfortunately the back wheels then went over him.

Pub names in the village like the Coach and Horses, remind us of those days, as does the Wagon and Horses for this takes us back to 'Herbert', a wagoner in the 12th century. He had a duty to provide carrying services for Ramsey Abbey, in Huntingdonshire to which Barton had been given by Bishop Eadnoth. For the journey to Ramsey, Herbert would receive a meat pasty, perhaps worth more than the penny he received for a London trip which entailed climbing Barton Hill.

Luton has long been important for the well-being of the village; in fact, the splendid recreation ground was a gift from Harry Arnold, a former Mayor of Luton. Industry's needs there have provided plenty of opportunities right from the days of hat-making. In 1815, a young Bedford widow with twins was so desperate for work she walked the 14 miles to Barton carrying one child, which she hid under a hedge, whilst she went back for the other one. The next day she carried both babies the last few miles to Luton.

🌿 BEDFORD

—— The same sweep of the Great Ouse that gives us the Embankment to enjoy must also have pleased a Saxon chief called Beda because here the river could be forded. There is still evidence to show the Saxons were here. Both St Peter's and St Mary's churches show traces from that period.

Fortunately Bedford has cared for its watery inheritance, like the treasured possession it is, enjoyed by residents and tourists alike. A bridge to replace the ford was essential and a charter granted to Simon de Beauchamp in the 1180s mentions Bedford Bridge and its chapel. Offerings could be made by grateful users of the bridge for its upkeep. This changed in 1331, when the chapel was either rebuilt or restored, because then a chaplain was appointed to collect money, on behalf of the mayor. This annoyed the sheriff who ejected the chaplain in 1332 and installed his own man, starting a dispute which was to last twelve years. Finally it was agreed that the mayor, bailiffs and goodmen of Bedford would get the money via the 'warden of the King's free chapel of St Thomas the Martyr on the bridge'. There was also a prison on the bridge for in 1671, after a damaging flood, it was agreed 'the prison upon the bridge shall be rebuilt'. At this time Bedford's famous son, John Bunyan, was in the County Gaol which stood on the corner of Silver Street and High Street.

The new Bedford Bridge was designed in 1810 by local architect John Wing. Money had to be borrowed to pay for it so a toll was necessary until 1835 to clear the debt. Just over the bridge, on the north side, stands the elegant Swan Hotel designed by the famous Henry Holland for the Duke of Bedford in 1794, which used the staircase from Houghton House at Ampthill, now a ruin. The Swan extends down the Embankment parallel with Castle Lane, which reminds us of the siege of Bedford Castle in 1224 when Henry III defeated Falkes de Breaute and hanged 80 of his men from the castle walls but spared him. The castle was then demolished but the mound remains.

Bedford had received its charter from Henry II in 1166 and members of Newnham Priory, where Priory Marina is sited, were soon teaching at a grammar school in the town. This stopped when Henry VIII dissolved the priory in 1541 and, had it not been for one man, the story of Bedford could have been very different. In 1566 Sir William Harpur endowed a grammar school in Bedford with 13 acres of land he bought in Holborn. He was a remarkable man; born in Bedford about 1496 he went to London where he was apprenticed to a City merchant. He rose to be master of the Merchant Taylor Company, became Sheriff of London, then Lord Mayor and was knighted in 1562. Shortly afterwards he helped found the Merchant Taylor School in the city.

At the beginning of the High Street was the house of William White whose son, William Hale White, was born in 1831. He was well educated and it was expected he would become an independent church minister. Nearer the time he acknowledged his religious doubts so joined the Civil Service instead and obtained a position in the Admiralty, which he supplemented by parliamentary journalism. He developed a style of writing noted for its clarity and form and started producing books under the pseudonym 'Mark Rutherford'. These were well received and some have a veiled Bedfordshire setting.

Another local boy who made good was James Howard, son of John Howard, once a jailer at the prison (see Clapham entry). Having had experience of the foundry business, he set up the Britannia Iron Works and manufactured the 'champion plough of England' from a design by a fellow Methodist from Wilstead. This enterprise brought new employment to the town and other opportunities.

Other manufacturing concerns came to Bedford in the following years and brickworks in the south took on many workers after 1945. Many of the town's pleasant buildings remain, and items of interest, like the golden bull over the clock in the High Street and figures around the plinth of the Howard and Bunyan statues, can still be admired. Some things have gone, like the old lunatic asylum, off Ampthill Road, which was another building designed by John Wing. We can read in *Reminiscences by the Honourable Grantley Berkeley* that in the 19th century a farmer, who was a patient there, saw a gentleman he recognised talking to the doctor. He was so convinced the visitor was enquiring about him he made a rapid recovery and later thanked the kind gentleman for getting him out.

BIDDENHAM

Called 'Bideham' in the Domesday Book, the 'ham' part of the name meaning home, this village retains its rural atmosphere even though just a stone's throw from Bedford.

The parish boundary follows the meandering route of the Great Ouse and separates the village from neighbouring Bromham. Here, spanning the water and extending right across the flood meadows, stands the local landmark – an impressive multi-arched bridge. In one form or another it has been here since at least 1227 when it appears in the records as 'Bideham Bridge.' In 1728, quite suddenly, it became 'Bromham Bridge', which it still is. Nobody seems to know how this happened especially as only four of its twenty-six arches are in that village.

Back in the annals of Biddenham, we find the name of Richard Boteler. He came from a working-class background, prospered in London, then through marriage to Grace Kirton acquired her family's manor. Their son William was Lord Mayor of London in 1515 and their grandson, also William, built the north aisle of Biddenham church in 1540. He became Sheriff of Bedford in 1588 and a year later was sitting as a Justice of the Peace with his neighbour, John Dyve. He was the son of the noble Sir Lewis Dyve of Bromham, and named his own son, born in 1599, Lewis, after his father.

It happened the two men fell out and John Dyve challenged William Boteler to a duel but he refused to fight. Biding his time, John Dyve gathered together nine men armed with swords and staves and they waited outside the church for their unprepared quarry. William Boteler and the four servants with him all suffered badly in the fracas and the conflict between the two men continued for some years, only ending by the wishes of Sir Lewis Dyve on his death bed in 1592. In due course the Civil War came and the two families fought on opposing sides: the Dyves were Royalists and the Botelers, Parliamentarians.

Justice in Biddenham was meted out on the gallows erected at Gallows Corner, a sharp bend in the road at the Bedford edge of the village. Crossroads here ensured the awesome contraption would be conspicuous and act as a deterrent. Executions were taking place as early as 1303 and then in 1605 we read that the notorious highwayman Gamaliel Ratsey was brought to Biddenham and dispatched.

It was not unusual for the family of a victim to celebrate after the hangman had done his job and a Luton family did it in style. First they threw a big party then presented each guest with a beautifully inscribed lace-maker's bobbin which read 'Hung on Biddenham Gallows – Matthias and William Lilley of Elstow'. By 1802 the old gallows were described as 'useless' and, after five centuries, were finally demolished. New gallows were already in operation at Bedford gaol on a regular basis.

BIGGLESWADE

The clue in the name is 'wade', where the river could be waded across, and 'Biggle' comes from the man who owned the land. It is a fertile area by the river Ivel and the settlement grew along the Great North Road, held by the crown at the time of the Domesday survey. It included three manors, Holme, Stratton, and Biggleswade, and aerial photography has now picked out a motte and bailey castle site.

Henry I granted the manors of Biggleswade and Holme to Lincoln Cathedral in 1132, with all the benefits plus a church; in return the Bishop would send a sable-lined gown to the King annually. Rights to a market and fair came in the 13th century. The River Ivel had a bridge across it from very early days – we learn that in 1308 the Bishop was offering indulgences in exchange for contributions. The river powered Biggleswade's mill, and later there were windmills. The last was brick built in 1860 and, at 70 feet high, the tallest in the county. It was a tower mill with the advantage that it could automatically turn into the wind and it worked until 1931.

Surprisingly, Biggleswade did not expand rapidly in spite of its advantageous position and it was still not considered a town by tax assessors in 1297. It had its share of crime and also failed in its duty as a 'hundred' to pursue villains afterwards. It was possible at this time for a criminal to seek sanctuary in the church and he could remain there for 40 days in all, as happened at St Andrew's; when the time was up he was allowed safe conduct from the church, dressed in sackcloth and carrying a cross, to be marched to the nearest dock by the coroner and put on a ship, never to return. It was not always the poor who were guilty of anti-social behaviour; the squirearchy got involved in a fracas at

The Market Square, Biggleswade

the sessions in 1437 when John Enderby of Biggleswade was attending and a dagger was drawn. Complaints were made to the King's Council by Enderby and Thomas Stratton, clerk of the peace at Biggleswade, supported by other signatories, but the perpetrator was well connected and nothing came of it.

A great fire in 1785 destroyed a large part of Biggleswade and left many homeless. It started in the yard of the Crown Inn and spread across the thatched roofs. The Sun Inn was spared, which must have pleased the Honourable John Byng, the diarist, for it was his favourite alehouse where he regularly drank his three pints daily plus half a bottle of brandy and liked the food as well. He admitted spending too much time in The Sun, and noted that a traveller, even if a peer, needs 'ever at his call a purse well lyned with coyne to pay for all'.

Inns at Biggleswade flourished because the Great North Road brought coaches through, but roads constantly needed repair so tollgates were built. However, to stop three times at three mile intervals to pay another toll only held up the traffic and encouraged some users to drive across fields to avoid the gates. Drovers faced difficulties with so many hold-ups and had to be skilful, just like the thief at Biggleswade market who managed to steal a large pig from a pen and get it out of the town undetected. At their peak in the 19th century, there were 15 coaches per day leaving the town centre for London, whilst slow-moving barges also brought trade to the town.

Steam eventually introduced auxiliary power into mills and the need for engines increased. One Biggleswade apprentice was Dan Albone who became an innovative mechanical designer, particularly well known for his work on bicycles. He developed safe machines for ladies and a practical tandem, but it was his racing machines that were in great demand, even overseas, particularly as he was winning prizes racing them. The river Ivel gave its name to his cycle works and, in due course, a tractor was developed here. Biggleswade keeps the memory of its famous son alive with a riverside picnic area and cycle stands made in the shape of bicycles which is fitting for a town so long associated with transport and the Great North Road.

BILLINGTON

This small community lies in pleasant countryside just south of Leighton Buzzard, not far from the Buckinghamshire border. It is an ancient place. Records show that an archery expert, or bowyer, was living here in 1297 and we know the church dates from the same period. It was rebuilt in Victorian times.

It was to this church of St Michael, after the First World War, that a battered cavalry-trumpet was brought which had once belonged to a trooper in the City of London Yeomanry. A notation simply said: 'This trumpet was carried to the fall of Jerusalem on December 9th 1917'. By itself the old trumpet was of little value, just a souvenir from yet another battle, but it was a reminder of a desert campaign which involved Lawrence of Arabia and captured the imagination of many, including the film makers.

General Allenby, who was responsible for liberating Jerusalem from the entrenched German and Turkish troops, was careful not to enter the Holy City as a conquering hero. Instead he left his horse at the Jaffa Gate and walked in with a dignity that was suitable for the occasion and accepted the surrender. At the same time, only a few miles from Billington, Lord Rosebery of Mentmore, a former Prime Minister, was grieving the loss of his son Neil, one of the young cavalry officers involved who never lived to see the victory.

Over its long period in St Michael's the old trumpet must have stimulated many thoughts from the young and adventurous to the older, more thoughtful members of the congregation. Although it survived great battles in the desert and the long journey home from Palestine, it lost out to a commonly held belief, some years ago, that nobody would steal from a church and its present whereabouts remain unknown.

BLUNHAM

———— This substantial village, hugging the river Ivel, has an ancient and attractive pinnacled church impressive enough to have two names, St James and St Edmund.

It was to this church in 1622 that the 7th Earl of Kent presented John Donne as rector even though he could not reside in the parish since he was already Dean of St Paul's – an appointment some people disagreed with because they believed he was primarily a careerist.

They had good reason to think this because John Donne had had an unusual life for a rector. He was born in 1572, the son of a prosperous ironmonger, and was educated at Oxford. He was not

Blunham

allowed to take a degree there, or at Cambridge, because he was a Catholic. So, with time on his hands, he travelled on the Continent with other young men, then became a law student at Lincoln's Inn. He was just 21 when his brother, Henry, was seized for harbouring a Catholic priest and died in prison soon afterwards. John was deeply disturbed by this and, renouncing his religion, went to sea. First he joined the Earl of Essex in the attack on Cadiz in 1596 then a year later was with Sir Walter Raleigh looking for Spanish treasure ships to capture off the Azores.

John was already a talented writer and his adventures on the high seas prompted him to record them in two poems, *The Storm* and *The Calm*. One of his shipmates was Thomas Egerton and, upon their return, he got John a job as secretary to his father, Sir Thomas, who held a crown appointment. Later John became a Member of Parliament for Brackley, which was a seat under Egerton control. At last his career seemed to be taking off. Then fate intervened – he fell in love with Anne More, Lady Egerton's niece. There was no possibility of John being acceptable to her family so the young couple eloped. Anne's father was so incensed he had John locked up in Fleet prison for a time and Sir Thomas Egerton instantly dismissed him.

Nobody would employ him in a responsible position again and times were hard when he had a growing family to support. Fortunately some of his in-laws quietly helped and friends supported them too, including his old Continental travelling companion and patron, Sir Robert Drury, and another generous colleague, Sir Henry Goodyer.

John continued to write but he had other talents not being used. One of his friends appealed to James I to help but the King would not budge from his conviction that John Donne was not suitable for confidential employment and suggested he joined the Church. To make this happen James I ordered Cambridge University to grant him a degree, which they did with a great deal of anger. John was ordained in 1615 – his fourteen years of enforced idleness finally over.

Two years later his beloved Anne died, giving birth to their twelfth child, so never lived to see him become Dean of St Paul's and be ranked by many as the finest preacher in the country. Blunham was looked after for him in his absence by a curate but John spent his holidays and any spare time in this peaceful part of Bedfordshire until he died in 1631.

BOLNHURST

The name of this small community on the Bedford to Kimbolton road crops up regularly in the annals of county history. Even the church has a legend attached to it.

St Dunstan's is named after a blacksmith who became the Archbishop of Canterbury after catching the devil by the nose with red-hot tongs. Apparently the devil had entered the smithy in the guise of a beautiful woman but cloven hoofs, where feet should have been, gave the game away.

A church plaque reminds us of the Francklin family who started as yeomen but were gentry by the 17th century when Sir William Francklin twice became Member of Parliament for Bedford. He died in debt, even owing money to his wine merchant, and it was left to the next Francklin to restore the family fortune by a more prudent lifestyle.

In 1888 the rector of St Dunstan's, Robert Atherton, described himself as a ploughboy, parson and poet. His odes were certainly different and his sense of humour always present. He wrote under the pseudonym 'Rupert Upperton" in a book called *Village Life and Feeling*. Of his lowly start in life he says:

> I am a ploughboy, bending forth with grace
> To turn my furrow as my horses pace ...
> I'm proud of my ploughing; but can't abide
> To praise myself with mighty commendation
> In what some say, Is quite beyond my station!

BROMHAM

Well known because of its place on the Great Ouse, its bridge of 26 arches and an ever popular mill, this village was home to W. H. Allen, the founder of the renowned Queens Engineering Works in Bedford a couple of miles away.

This great entrepreneur arrived in 1894. He was on his way to Derby, seeking potential factory sites, when he saw through the carriage window 13 acres for sale at Bedford. Fortunately for the local economy, he bought those instead. It was the turbines built by his company that were used on the mighty *Titanic*. The beautiful residence, set in extensive grounds, that W. H. Allen built for himself at the end of the 19th century became the Bromham Hospital of the 20th century – a welcome provider of employment at the time.

A much older building was Bromham Hall, a private residence, where past lords of the manor, like the Dyves or the Trevors, had once lived. Of the Dyves we know they were Royalists in the Civil War and when Parliamentarian soldiers arrived and surrounded the house to capture Sir Lewis Dyve, he dived into the river in true cavalier fashion, swam to the other side and got to Nottingham to continue the fight. Later he was caught and put into the King's Bench Prison in London. There he crawled down a filthy latrine chute and dropped into the Thames to make another watery escape.

The Dyves sold Bromham Hall to Thomas Trevor in 1708. He was a Chief Justice who was elevated to the peerage in 1712, the first ever to be honoured in this way. By 1776 another Trevor had become Viscount Hampden. Various memorials to the family are displayed in the parish church of St Owen but the most significant has to be a library donated by Thomas, Lord Trevor in 1740 and originally kept in the 'Priest Room' over the south porch, but now safely in the County Archive.

❧ CADDINGTON

—— Spreading across the high ground between Luton and Dunstable this large village, called 'Cadendone' in the Domesday survey, is world famous archaeologically speaking because of what was found by Worthington Smith, a 19th century Dunstable antiquarian. He discovered that the same clay that produced the nice Caddington Grey bricks also concealed Stone Age items of immense interest.

Numerous implements were found in various stages of completion and the site appeared to be the workshop of an ancient flint-knapper. As Worthington Smith held the Stone Age tools in his hands he must have been acutely aware they had not been touched since fashioned by a prehistoric man. The objects went to local museums as well as the British Museum and in 1894 Worthington Smith wrote his book, *Man, the Primeval Savage,* well illustrated by his own drawings. His visits to Caddington had been almost daily over several years and he had painstakingly delved into at least half a dozen clay pits for his great finds.

In 1971-2 an American-funded team set out to retrace the steps of the old pioneer and, though they found no more artefacts, they made other valuable discoveries all adding to our knowledge of the Stone Age. By then the former clay pits had been filled in as brick-making had long ceased, ending another facet of village history.

CARDINGTON

The huge hangars are a constant reminder of the ill-fated R101 airship; so is the ensign that strangely survived the inferno and was brought to St Mary's church, where the 46 victims of the 1930 disaster rest in peace. During World War II thousands of RAF personnel first came to Cardington Airfield which was their reception centre.

Long before, the village was known as the home of John Howard, the famous 18th century prison reformer, whose epitaph in Russia encapsulates his life's work: 'Whosoever thou art, thou standest at the grave of thy friend'. Howard was related to the Whitbreads who also lived in the village, which was to form part of their estate.

From this era came John Smeaton, retained by Samuel Whitbread for bridge-building and for work on an old mill. He already had a reputation for excellence, having rebuilt Eddystone Lighthouse off Plymouth in stone after two wooden ones had failed. Having designed several water-mills, he published his findings in *Powers of Wind and Water* and was elected to the Royal Society. Fire was always a danger in mills and the one he built at Cardington in 1786 burned down in 1823. Undaunted, William Whitbread had it rebuilt within a year. Again, in 1840, it burned down and was rebuilt within the same year. This time it stood for almost a century before it was demolished by Bedford Corporation.

No entry on Cardington would be complete without a mention of the celebrated diarist from Southill, the Hon John Byng, who wrote of it in 1789 as: 'A village of much neatness, with all the houses so smart, and the green so nicely planted: to add to which there was a little fair, and a stall, and a Turnabout to make the children sick after gingerbread.'

CARLTON

This village and its tiny partner Chellington each had a church built. From one of them, St Mary's at Carlton, now the parish church, we find in the 17th century parishioners getting rid of their rector, William Pargiter, because he liked a drink – or two. The other, St Nicholas' church, became a useful social centre.

A real character that emerges in the 18th century was Carlton's rector, Benjamin Foster, who fortunately kept a diary of his life and times. He notes down in 1729 that he decided William Allen needed to give blood to relieve his pleurisy but, after being well

Carlton High Street in 1978

blooded twice, there was no improvement so more was taken but this time he died. We also read about Benjamin's five year old son John 'who fell backwards into the pottage pot, just as it was taken boiling off the fire for dinner, but was taken out immediately by the maid. The fleshy part of his backside was miserably scolded.'

Whatever treatment the child received from Benjamin must have worked for he lived until nearly 60. It seems that a Mrs Gibbons had little faith in Benjamin's cures for when she felt she was dying with stomach ache her messenger was sent all the way to Arlesey for a doctor only to discover he had gone to Bath. After a visit to Bedford with his wife in 1730, Benjamin faithfully records items of gossip they picked up, such as 'that a pipe-maker called Branklin (that had hanged honest John) was poisoned the day before by his wife who put arsenic in his pudding. She ran away as soon as she had done it.' We also get a picture of Benjamin as a caring husband and father when his daughter, coming home from London in 1735, had been collected by her mother from Bedford in a chaise. 'God send them a good journey', he notes for posterity to reflect on.

Generally Benjamin seems to have enjoyed a good relationship with his flock, quite different from the trouble Carlton had endured some years earlier when a new Baptist minister, John Greenwood, came to the parish. He made it clear he was in favour of infant baptism and immediately fell foul of deacon William Bithrey who, with supporters, loudly demanded baptism for adults only. It was an impasse and when the new minister tried to lay down the law, Bithrey 'fell into a wicked passion'. The discord dragged on, with other churches trying to mediate, but it was only when John Greenwood left the village that peace returned.

CHALGRAVE

—— This is an ancient place which joins with Tebworth and Wingfield to make one parish, well spread out around Toddington. Once there were houses near the lonely 13th century church and one belonged to Nigel Loring, Lord of the Manor and soldier of fortune. He joined Edward III in his attempt to re-establish England's place in western Europe and was on one of the 147 ships in the fleet that sailed across the Channel in 1340 to fight our first sea battle with the French.

Waiting at the harbour of Sluys were 190 French ships and 35,000 soldiers. However, two out of every three of Edward's vessels contained archers and when they were close enough to the 'forest of masts' this weapon proved as decisive then as it would in future battles. The struggle was hard fought – one English ship lost every single man to stoning from aloft – but at the end of the day it was a rout, with 166 French ships either destroyed or captured.

For his part in this important action, Nigel Loring was knighted and six years later was with the King at Crecy, where once again English longbowmen won the day. This time 17 year-old Edward, the Black Prince, took part to prove himself in battle and Nigel was at his side. He became a comrade in arms to the Prince and was with him through his subsequent French and Spanish campaigns. In the meantime Edward III decided to form his knights into a fraternity, like King Arthur had, and the Order of the Garter was initiated. Nigel became one of the 26 chosen men and his stall plate was placed in St George's Chapel, Windsor, on the same side as that of the Black Prince.

As he had become wealthy over his years of soldiering, Nigel was able to support Dunstable Priory with various gifts and it was his wish that he be buried there. He died in 1386, the last of the Lorings, having only two daughters. To one of these he left his land and to the other the house that once stood near All Saints, Chalgrave.

CHICKSANDS AND CAMPTON

—— Its military presence and ancient priory make Chicksands a better known place than Campton but the two have always been closely associated. Campton is an interesting village with attractive houses and pleasant cottages leading to crossroads and the church, All Saints', which has seen changing times in the community since Henry III was on the throne, though restoration work in the 19th century was responsible for its present day appearance. Built of sandstone, with a tall tower and prominent battlements, it is a handsome building. The influence of the Osborne/Osborn family from Chicksands Priory pervades the chapel inside which was built by them in the mid

17th century. Here many members of that notable family were laid to rest and their family crest, a hand on a shield, is seen here as well as on cottages that they built in the village.

Close to All Saints' is the manor house. This impressive black and white building, showing through trees at the end of the drive, was built in 1591 in the attractive Tudor style and belonged to the Ventris family. During the Civil War a Roundhead fired a shot through the window at Royalist, Sir Charles Ventris, but only damaged some oak panelling. In the 18th century the manor was sold to Sir George Osborn of Chicksands Priory which before the Dissolution had belonged to the Gilbertine Order who had built it during the 12th century.

Being English and enclosing both males and females, probably made this order unique. The regime was severe and a story is told that when a nun named Rosata fell in love with a canon and got pregnant, she was first made to witness his execution then was entombed alive in the cloisters by order of the Prior. Her ghost has regularly been observed, apparently passing the spot where a plaque reads:

By virtue guarded and manners graced
Here, alas is fair Rosata placed.

CLAPHAM

The road to Northamptonshire cuts through this large village whose straggling High Street runs parallel to the Great Ouse flowing down to Bedford a couple of miles away. Perhaps it was for protection from waterborne invaders that the Saxons built their lofty tower, which with its Norman extension is over 80 feet high and rightly the pride of Clapham.

Inside St Thomas' church, which it became, another Thomas is remembered. He was Thomas Taylor, the 17th century lord of the manor, whose widow Ursula founded a charity to provide a much needed apprenticeship for village youngsters. Their ancient manor house did not survive but another great house was built in 1872 for James Howard, founder of the Britannia Iron Works in Bedford. The builder was talented Blunham man, John Usher, who had worked for the Howard family on other projects.

The entrepreneurial spirit of the Howard family probably came from old John Howard, who was once a jailer at Bedford but got the sack for putting the prisoners to work on some land he owned rather than have them stay idle. Later the authorities built a treadmill to keep prisoners active, so his idea was acted on.

CLIFTON

—— This village give its name to the 'hundred' it was part of and was the meeting place for the other nine villages who met monthly to deal with local matters. Some years ago these old meetings were revived by the launch of a Clifton Hundred Festival.

Being near the river Ivel, Clifton had a mill for which it paid 150 eels annually to the lord of the manor and by the 19th century it also benefited from the Ivel Navigation Scheme. One disadvantage of this, for market gardeners anyway, was that the slow-moving craft allowed the lightermen to slip ashore and help themselves to crops but it also enabled the constable to get from Clifton to Stanford Lock and be waiting for the thieves.

The parish church of All Saints has watched over the changes since the 14th century and, when common land existed for grazing, the rector kept a bull and a boar for parish use, under his control to avoid disputes. Anther incumbent, Reverend S. S. Oliver, established a school at his own expense in 1807 and to fit in with everybody's needs he had a three-shift system, closing finally at 8pm.

Children at Clifton were sent to plait school, as happened all across the county because it was a chance to earn a few pence making the straw plait for the hat trade. Unfortunately, conditions were often poor and one cottage in the village, used as a plait school in 1871, had fifty-one children crowded into a room only ten feet square without proper ventilation.

As there were once six public houses in the village it seems it was a popular place for a drink. This was particularly so in 1820 at George IV's coronation where local landowners provided every man in the village with one quart of beer, the women folk one pint and children half a pint.

CLOPHILL

As traffic slows at a busy roundabout and crossroads on the A6 trunk road between Bedford and Luton, we see the Flying Horse where travellers have been made welcome since coaching days. It is here we find a shady village green, fronted by ancient and attractive cottages and a relic from the days of instant justice, the village lock-up. Here drunkards sobered up, wife beaters cooled off and others awaited transport to Bedford gaol.

Clophill spreads eastwards, the narrow river Flit flowing in the same direction eventually passing the outlying village boundary near Beadlow as well as the motte and bailey remains at Cainhoe. There was a manor here from Norman times for we read that Peter de St Croix, his 16 year old son and nearby cottagers all died of the plague which visited the community in 1349, no doubt influencing future development.

Extensive woodland around Clophill makes this an attractive area particularly if coupled with that part of the High Street between St Mary's and the green where some of the more substantial properties were built, including a nearby 13th century mill. At the eastern end of the village we find a pumping station that was built in 1907 to supply Ampthill with water, a distance of 4½ miles. In 1922 it was decided that when there was a fire in Ampthill a man should be dispatched to Clophill in the fire-station's vehicle to contact the manager of the waterworks and get the pumps going – a far cry from a mobile 'phone.

COCKAYNE HATLEY

The name is almost lyrical and came about by combining that of a lord of the manor, John Cockayne, with the village named Hatley. His ancient house is gone but records remain and we read of its invasion in 1470 by ten men, some with drawn swords and others with bows and arrows.

They forced their way inside looking for one John Wareyn who, they said, had stolen two silver shillings. It seems the constable had been reluctant to arrest the man so they had taken it upon themselves. John Cockayne took them to court over their violent behaviour towards his servants who had tried to keep them out. They pleaded that they had 'only placed their hands gently on the said servants and pushed them quietly to one side'.

The best known of the Cockayne family was Henry Cockayne Cust, who was also the rector of the parish church of St John the Baptist which had stood as a village landmark since the 13th century – the resting place of his ancestors. In 1830 Henry restored the dilapidated church, making it the attractive building we see today with its lofty pinnacled tower and battlements overlooking the Cambridgeshire border.

Wanting to beautify the inside as well, Henry scoured the Continent and in Belgium bought the most exquisite carved church furniture from an old abbey. The 17th century baroque wood carvings on the choir stalls and backs make this collection special but there is plenty more. Also there are church brasses thought to be amongst the best in the county. Henry Cockayne Cust left us richer by his efforts.

COLMWORTH

An agricultural area, north-east of Bedford, it has been called 'Cold Colmworth' because it gets bleak in winter, like so many rural areas. Its church spire is an impressive landmark, advertising the ancient church of St Denis. Inside there is a bold and beautiful statement, by way of a monument and poem, from a widow who could not be consoled, to her young husband sadly departed. The couple were Sir William Dyer and his Lady and their seven children are included in the sculpture.

One flamboyant figure who cut quite a figure for himself was curate of St Denis', Timothy Richard Matthews, who preferred to preach out of doors in true evangelistic style. He would often use a trumpet to get a congregation together and crowds flocked to hear him. He married Ann Fielding, from Eaton Socon, whose two sisters and brother had become Mormons in America. He became chaplain to the workhouse and would fill the chapel to overflowing. Sadly, he became a victim of typhus fever and died quite suddenly, still comparatively young. His followers buried him in Bedford but later his body was brought back to Colmworth to rest in peace with his wife at St Denis' where he first learned to preach.

Many people remember going to Colmworth school, under the shadow of the great spire, reciting their playful ditty:

If Colmworth spire was twenty times higher
I would take off my shoe and jump over it.

COPLE

An eye-catching former tollgate house along the Bedford to Sandy road stands at the Cople turn. It is one of only two left in the county, most being lost through road-widening schemes. This particular example, with windows in its porch to watch for traffic, was erected in the late 18th century by the Turnpike Trust to maintain the road.

In the village centre is the parish church of All Saints, mainly from the 15th century. It has some interesting brasses including those of the Launcelyns who were the family that, through marriage, brought the Lukes to Cople. Sir Samuel Luke was the best known, being the most prominent Parliamentarian in the county. He was a man of action even though still a serving Member of Parliament. In 1643 he raised a Bedfordshire troop of dragoons but they were destroyed by Prince Rupert.

Newport Pagnell was the garrison town for this area and Sir Samuel became Governor there with sixteen hundred troops to command. He had his share of troubles, mainly over supplies and getting money from the counties, especially his own. Once he complained about having two men with only one pair of breeches between them who had to take turns staying in bed. He also had to suffer the loss of garrison funds from two thieving officers.

Although the general image of a Puritan is one of drabness, Sir Samuel was a very colourful character which reflected in his clothes, especially the long scarlet cloak he wore. In Cople church at this time John Gwin, the local vicar, was expounding Royalist views to the congregation which eventually cost him his living plus a fine of one hundred pounds and a spell in Newgate prison. As soon as possible after his release he emigrated to Virginia, USA.

Another preacher, John Wesley, visited Cople in 1766 and found the people 'the most lively in all the little societies in Bedfordshire'. It was a different matter in 1757 when the authorities wanted details of every man aged between 17 and 50 to make up a militia. Hundreds demonstrated against this, knowing full well that whilst they were serving their wives and families would suffer hardship. The constables were too intimidated to continue the count. False rumours about overseas service did not help.

As well as the tollgate house, Cople has another rarity, a bier-house. This quaint little building once housed the bier, or handcart, used for transporting coffins from the houses to the church. The village might also be unique in having a vicar, H. E. Havergal, who with the help of his musical family built his own church organ.

CRANFIELD

—— When we think of this village in the west of the county we automatically associate its name with Cranfield University which has long enjoyed a reputation for excellence. It has had a couple of name changes since its arrival in 1946, following a wartime decision by Sir Stafford Cripps' department for a specialised aeronautical college after the war. Cranfield had all the facilities needed and its initial equipment included many

The centre of Cranfield, 1974

items from Germany even an infamous V2 rocket.

All the open spaces, including the airfield, were covered by forest originally but, in a clearing, beautiful cranes used to fly in from the fens where they had arrived from abroad. The place was first called 'Cran-feld' because of these welcome visitors and then 'Cranfield'. Sadly, cranes only continued visiting until the 17th century and are now found just in zoos.

Initially the land belonged to Alwyn who gave it to the great abbey at Ramsey but not much changed before the Domesday survey of 1086 when it was recorded it had wooded land which could sustain a thousand pigs. Ramsey Abbey held Cranfield until the Dissolution then Edward VI gave it to his half-sister, Princess Elizabeth. The first church at Cranfield was built by the monks but a more substantial one replaced it and the present St Peter and St Paul's is from the 13th century with Norman traces.

DEAN

——— This village, with an Upper and Lower part, is at the county's northern tip, close to where three counties converge. This made it convenient for poachers and, in 1251, a dozen men from Dean were seen in Northamptonshire armed with bows and arrows chasing game with greyhounds. They escaped but Alexander of Wootton was not so lucky. He came to Dean in 1312 looking for buried treasure and was apprehended because he did not have a royal warrant to do so. He explained that he never found anything anyway. Had he been a local man the authorities would have kept an eye on him to see 'if he carried himself more richly in clothing, food and drink and the like'. In case Alexander had concealed any treasure before being caught they stuck him in Bedford prison for the next three years.

Some interesting people have been connected with Dean over the years, including Captain Henry Bayntun of HMS *Leviathan*, whose granddaughter married locally and brought with her his log-books of the Battle of Trafalgar. On that fateful day in 1805 the *Leviathan* and *Neptune*, two average size ships, faced the formidable *Santissima Trinidad*, the largest fighting ship afloat, the flagship of the Spanish Admiral. After a fierce engagement the enemy ship was destroyed and *Leviathan's* captain later became Admiral Sir Henry Bayntun, clearly a man with the Nelson touch.

In 1702 a village benefactor, Joseph Neale, endowed a school for 20 poor boys and it was decided they would use All Saints as a schoolroom and the rector as schoolmaster. On top of that he would have to preach a sermon to the governors every Whit-Sunday and they 'had to take note of his behaviour and the boys' improvement'. It was bad behaviour that cost an ill-fated burglar his life in Dean in 1317 for he had got a ladder and was trying to enter Maude Belle's house to steal a ham. Apparently she surprised him and he slipped, breaking his neck in the fall.

DUNSTABLE

Whole books have been written about this town which figured so prominently in English history. We learned at school about the great priory being founded by the first King Henry and dissolved by the last and of Catherine of Aragon being brought from Ampthill and told she was divorced.

This is a town in which to linger, for the past is all around, from ancient inns, like the Sugar Loaf which reminds us that 80 coaches a day once came through here, to beautiful almshouses erected and endowed by local benefactors.

In the dominating hills, burial grounds have given up their secrets, gruesome at times, but always interesting, and Maiden-Bower Avenue links us with the huge Bronze Age camp that was here. The Icknield Way existed before the Romans came to cross it with their undeviating Watling Street and give us the only Roman settlement in the county, Durocobrivae, which came to nothing.

These crossroads that have both pleased and plagued us made a market feasible to Henry I and so the town began. Royalty and their entourages descended three times in the mid 14th century, twice for tournaments, which brought prosperity to the town – though a great deal of expense for the provider of the venue and the fare, John Durant, a rich merchant.

Later came the Dissolution, and when royalty stopped visiting Dunstable's status suffered. The sheriff of the county claimed entry and then, in 1540, when the town constable tried to stop him evicting a local man from his house, he had the constable put in the stocks and his supporters taken to Bedford prison. Not long afterwards Dunstable was being administered by the bailiff of Ampthill.

The High Street, Dunstable, showing the Chews Grammar School of 1719

It was a time of change – the old priory church became a beautiful parish church instead. The straw hat trade got established and by 1689 it was reckoned a thousand families depended on it for a living in and around the town, so an Act to encourage the wearing of woollen hats to help sheep farmers was vigorously opposed. By the 20th century it was the surfeit of female workers, no longer required in the hat trade, that influenced A. C. Sphinx Spark Plug Company, for example, to choose Dunstable for its new factory in 1934, which was quite an impressive addition to High Street North. It provided regular employment for over 60 years and at its peak in 1979 more than 2,000 people were on the payroll. Other major firms came, including vehicle manufacturers, making Dunstable a boom town, but times change and the next phase in the town's long history begins in a new millennium.

DUNTON

Close to both Biggleswade and the eastern border, this village has caused some odd comments to be made in the records. For instance it it mentioned that Cecily Woodward 'had petticoats of red and russet' and a church warden once pinned a notice to the door, before a vestry meeting, which said 'if none attends, I shall proceed as I think proper'. Still at the church, in

The pub and the church shape the centre of Dunton

1645 it seemed that Elizabeth Bates changed her mind at the altar on her wedding day for we read that she and George Richards 'were begun to be married November 18th but then her being unwilling to go forward their marriage was consummated the next day'.

Silently witnessing changing fortunes since the 14th century stands St Mary Magdalene's church whose steeple fell down in 1660. Fifty years later nothing had happened, then finally, after two centuries, the Victorians took the task in hand and a brand new steeple was built, quite distinctive from the rest of the church. In 1717 an added inducement to attend church on a Sunday was the distribution of free bread by the Reverend Peter Bamford.

The Quakers were quite strong in Dunton, as many as forty being recorded in 1669. Since such meetings were unlawful an Act was passed allowing one third of any fine imposed to be paid to informers. Since the Quakers refused to pay fines for their beliefs, their goods and chattels were distrained until, not unusually, there was nothing left to take. Faith was sorely tried in those days before the Toleration Acts.

EATON BRAY

——— It is hard to imagine a great castle being built in this pleasant place below Dunstable Downs but William de Cantilupe, the baron who held Eaton at the time, must have felt the need for protection in those turbulent years. By some it was seen as a threat to the locality and possibly to the King, but, as that was King John, who had just been forced to sign the Magna Carta, perhaps the baron was right to be cautious.

The second part of the village name, Bray, came much later when Sir Reginald Bray acquired the manor through his position as treasurer to Henry VII. He was very involved in the King's passion for building a chapel in Westminster Abbey and in rebuilding St George's Chapel, Windsor, where his monogram can be found. He shared his position as financial minister to the King with an archbishop and both were seen to be responsible for an intended tax increase to fund a military operation planned by the King.

So opposed were the people to tax increases that 15,000 men

marched from Cornwall, led by Lord Audley and supported by a lawyer, Thomas Flamank, and a blacksmith, Michael Joseph. They camped on Blackheath and demanded that the King dismiss both Sir Reginald Bray and the archbishop for wrongly advising him. Far from being intimidated Henry VII called out his troops and defeated the rebels. He then hanged the three ringleaders and sent the rest home with a warning. Sir Reginald Bray was given a further honour to crown his illustrious career, which ended with his death in 1503. All his estates passed to Sir Edmund Bray who became the first Lord Bray and whose wife Jane bore him ten daughters and just one son. It is her brass that was placed in the parish church of St Mary in 1558.

Perhaps the best known detail of St Mary's is the south door which is impressively covered in the wrought iron scroll-work of Thomas of Leighton, the 13th century craftsman responsible for the screen around Queen Eleanor's tomb in Westminster Abbey. Also in the church are two long poles with hooks on the end for pulling off the thatch from cottages if they caught fire. This was always a hazard and the arrival of steam engines to drive farm machinery must have caused apprehension. A farmer in the village who used a new threshing machine in the 19th century was not impressed. He said so much corn was left in the straw that the ricks later turned as green as meadows.

EGGINGTON

Eggington is an enclave of interest off the busy A4012 just a stone's throw from Leighton Buzzard. The road into the village winds past Eggington House whilst cattle flourish in green meadows that stretch down to Manor Farm. An old school building, with a bell fixed roof high, was built in 1880 and lasted until 1983 as a school, then put to good use as a village hall.

Along the High Street is a sign to Church Walk and it was here, until 1950, that Harry Edwards and Sons had their carpenter's shop which had enjoyed a reputation for craftsmanship for over a century. They also made coffins and the story goes that one customer had his coffin lined with lead with another wood lining inside that. Altogether a staggering weight. On the other side stands St Michael and All Angels' church which in the 14th century was a chapel of ease, under All Saints', Leighton

Buzzard, and of the two bells in the tower, one is engraved 'Zave our King 1622 + God', which presumably was the engraver's way of saying 'God save our King 1622'.

 ## ELSTOW

——— Bypassed in recent years, peace has returned to this famous village and visitors can again walk in the streets where John Bunyan played as a lad under the shadow of the mighty abbey church, where his journey to salvation began.

Only ruins remain where the abbey once stood but its founding in 1076 has all the drama, passion and intrigue of a Shakespeare play and it all began because William the Conqueror wanted to pacify the large and restless population by getting one of their leaders, Waltheof, to marry a Norman girl.

The girl he chose was Judith, his own niece, who had many fine qualities but none which endeared her to Waltheof who was ardently anti-Norman. Pressure was brought to bear: he either married Judith or lost his rank and status as earl. Waltheof chose marriage, as the lesser of two evils, thus publicly acknowledging William as his king, but inwardly nothing had changed.

Within a few months of the marriage fighting broke out in York and Waltheof rushed to join in. As a result of the action over a hundred Norman soldiers were killed before the revolt was crushed. He was brought before William and was very lucky to be granted a pardon.

For a while, Waltheof settled down to life with Judith and three daughters were born but, sadly for Judith, the respite was not to last and eventually she found Waltheof once more embroiled in a plot to overthrow William. It seems this time she actually persuaded him against such folly because he suddenly left his fellow conspirators and confessed his erring ways to William, expecting another pardon so he could get on with life as a dutiful husband.

Unfortunately William had had enough of his doubtful allegiance and sent him to Winchester to be tried for treason. Judith pleaded with her uncle to spare his life but he allowed the law to take its course and Waltheof was found guilty and beheaded.

The execution made a martyr out of him but an ogre out of

Judith and she was ostracised from then on. In her grief she founded Elstow Abbey which was seen by many as an atonement for betraying her husband. The abbey flourished until dissolved by Henry VIII in 1535 but the church remained and at its Norman font in 1628 John Bunyan received his infant blessing.

EVERSHOLT

—— Any village whose name makes the pleasant anagram 'The Lovers' must be a nice place and Eversholt is certainly that. Set in a picture postcard location next to Woburn Park, the village was swallowed up when the 4th Duke of Bedford expanded his estate. As well as the central area around the 14th century church of John the Baptist, where cricket matches are played on the green, there are 14 'Ends', if all are counted. One is called Witts End which might indicate a visitor's feeling if searching for an address.

In its earlier history Eversholt, or Eofors Halt, meaning 'boars wood', was given to Princess Elizabeth in 1550 by her half-brother, Edward VI, but in the 14th century it was one of the Grey family's possessions. From this period we learn that Helen Sturmound was a scold but the rector was much worse for he shot arrows from the rectory at men coming to arrest him.

At lot of things happened to Eversholt in the 19th century. Sir Gilbert Scott restored the church and afterwards Edward Aveling Green brought his talent to bear with beautiful wall-paintings and wood-carvings. This remarkable man was born in Woburn in 1842, a younger brother of Colonel John Green of Ampthill Brewery. He started in engineering but gave it up for art and, after years of study at home and in Italy, he opened a studio in London.

Fortunately he had a sister in Eversholt and spent a few months every year at her home called Berrystead. Eventually he came to stay in the village but was already too elderly to climb on ladders and platforms while adorning the parish church as he planned so he skilfully painted the pictures on sections of canvas which were fixed to the walls. He also carved a fine wooden statuette of John the Baptist as well as an oak reredor depicting the Last Supper. Finally he created the impressive bronze figure of St Michael for the village war memorial. Edward died at the good old age of 88 leaving us a legacy of his artistic achievement.

EVERTON

Just past Sandy in the east of the county, this ancient village, whose name means 'boar farm', has a parish church that goes back to Norman times and a few skeletons in the cupboard. To compensate for these there have been some well-loved vicars at the church of St Mary like the Reverend Robert Green who, out of his own pocket, bought prayer books for 20 children and also paid the clerk two shillings a week to teach them to sing the psalms. This was something of a generous innovation for singing was not encouraged in many churches in 1724.

One of Everton's not so nice people was a judge, Sir Humphrey Winche, who sentenced nine hapless women to death at Leicester in 1616 for witchcraft. In this piece of barbarism he would have had the approval of James I who was terrified of witches, believing they once sent a storm to sink a ship he was on. Some of the accusations Sir Humphrey Winche heard were of crimes impossible to commit, which was frequently the case during this sad episode in our history. A bold monument to Sir Humphrey was erected in St Mary's in 1625 showing him with

Everton

his hand on a book in the company of cherubs.

Another skeleton in Everton's cupboard was John Tiptoft, Earl of Worcester, who was born in the village in 1427. He first went to Oxford then studied Latin in Italy where he mingled with the most learned men of the day. An ardent Yorkist, he found favour back home with Edward IV and, in turn, became Constable of England, Governor of Ireland, Chief Justice then Treasurer of the Realm. He was admitted to the Order of the Garter and it seemed his power knew no bounds.

His name was soon to be feared. Lancastrians were shown no mercy during this reign of terror and he earned the nickname 'Butcher of England' after apprehending 20 noblemen trying to leave the country. He not only hanged them all but had them drawn and quartered then their remains impaled on spikes, something he had learned in Italy.

There was public revulsion for this bloodthirsty exhibition and as soon as circumstances changed and the Lancastrians ruled he was the first one they came looking for. He tried disguising himself but was given away and captured when he climbed a tall tree to hide. The prosecutor at his trial happened to be a man whose father and brother had been victims so the outcome was never in doubt. So many people were trying to lynch him at his public execution they had to postpone it for a day, but then succeeded. An observer noted that in one stroke the axeman cut off more learning than was left in the heads of all the surviving nobility.

EYEWORTH

—— A bolt of lightning on a stormy night in 1967 demolished the steeple of the parish church of All Saints and, as there were insufficient funds to rebuild it, the village did the next best thing, they had a smaller steeple built more in keeping with the size of the community. Perhaps the same fate robbed the village of its windmill; we know there was one there in 1276 because we read of the foolish customer who was so busy harassing the lad in charge he got caught up in the cogs with fatal results.

A good picture of life in the village from the 19th century was given in a series of letters published in the *Bedfordshire Magazine* in the 1950s about 91 year old William Fielding. He was the eldest of a family of seventeen and recalled starting work on a farm in 1870 at nine years old and working all day, six days a week, for two shillings.

In 1887 he climbed a ladder to proudly hang the Union Jack on the church tower marking Queen Victoria's Jubilee and, later, started going away each year, with his scythe over his shoulder, on hay cutting trips. At one place he worked there were tennis courts nearby and he could fill his pockets with lost tennis balls. When he returned to Eyeworth he would march down the street throwing tennis balls to children who had been waiting for him.

William learned about wood and became a sawyer working in his saw pit making fences and gates and repairing barns, and sometimes a coffin would emerge from this woodyard. He spent his long life doing useful work in the place where he was born and a picture was taken of him sitting outside his cottage. It is filed away for posterity whilst he rests in peace after a contented life.

FELMERSHAM

The Great Ouse sweeps around this pleasant village and makes a shape that could be said to resemble a dog's head as it meanders south to Bedford. Various bronze objects excavated locally show that this river site was also popular with our early ancestors.

Whoever journeys to Felmersham has a pleasure in store. First there is the church of St Mary, described as the 'Cathedral of North Bedford' with good reason for it is large enough to grace any town. It is also a really beautiful church from every angle, but particularly the west front when viewed through the attractive lychgate. For a church of such splendour it was built in a surprisingly short time, only twenty years, between 1220 and 1240, of Early English design and has long been accepted as the finest of its type in the county.

Right outside St Mary's a huge tithe barn was built in the 15th century, in stone in keeping with the village which, together with the church, was held by Trinity College, Cambridge. In more recent times this became dilapidated and might have been lost forever but at the last minute was saved for posterity and transformed into dwelling houses of character retaining the ancient name.

Felmersham church and tithe barn in 1970

Until the 19th century the river close by had to be crossed by a ford and a bridge was only built after public subscription in 1818 had raised enough money. This was not without its problems – by 1819 two arches crashed down and in 1823 'the greatest flood that ever was known' knocked the parapet to pieces.

Like many villages, Felmersham has its legend. It concerns the pub sign of the Six Ringers which showed only five church bells. Apparently a jealous monk and helpers from Odell stole a bell from St Mary's one night for their church but it was too heavy for the boat and it sank, taking St Mary's sixth bell to the bottom.

FLITTON

This mid-county village gave us the Flitt Hundred in the 11th century, and down Brook Lane, near the church, we find the river Flitt which, at one time, fed the water-mill at the adjacent hamlet of Greenfield.

The Brook Lane area buzzed with police activity during World War II after a murder had been committed which shocked the community. Someone had clubbed a poor farm worker to death in woods leading to Flitwick, for a paltry thirty shillings. The police set up their operation at the White Hart pub, opposite the church, but in spite of their efforts the killer was never found.

Flitton's parish church of St John the Baptist was built by the de Greys of Wrest Park in the 15th century and they also built the mausoleum where the Duke of Kent and various earls and other members of this noble family rest in peace. It is one of the finest groups of monuments anywhere and when Hugh Walpole visited he referred to them as 'ten sumptuous monuments'. A funeral of a de Grey could be a big event with people lining the streets and often the church was draped in black.

As the de Grey estate expanded, land in the area was quickly purchased, sometimes it seems at a bargain price. When the Countess of Kent bought land at Flitton from John Pearles in 1679 he agreed that if in future he sold any more land adjoining hers she need only pay the same price. The de Greys wielded power and influence in the county for six generations and were highly respected. During the Napoleonic Wars when food prices rocketed deer were slaughtered at Wrest Park to feed the poor. When they spent time at their town house in London the vicars of Flitton and Clophill would vie with each other to be chosen as their local correspondent.

A local yeoman family of some standing in the 17th century were the Beaumonts and when Thomas Beaumont married the daughter of a gentleman in 1700 he owned over 100 acres of land. Fifty-one years later a highwayman was shot and buried near Beaumont land after a stake had been driven through his body. Eventually a tree grew which they called Beaumonts or Bowman's tree and somehow the belief spread that if people nailed a hair from their head onto the tree as Flitton church clock struck midnight they would get protection from ague, quite a common disease at the time. Judging by the nails found in the tree when it came down there were quite a few believers.

By contrast an epitaph at Flitton, reflecting on the life of Lady Joan Hart, who died in 1673, ends by saying, 'a pity so much goodness should ever die'.

Flitwick

Dwarfing Ampthill, its once larger neighbour, Flitwick now enjoys town status itself whilst retaining a nucleus of antiquity around Church Lane. Here timber-framed houses line the way to a large lychgate, marking an imposing entrance to St Peter and St Paul's which, like many churches, developed over the centuries.

As early as 1263 Canon Richards was being presented to Flitwick by Dunstable Priory but, soon afterwards, the village received the prior himself who had been deposed for being extravagant with funds. He arrived with a servant plus a regular allowance of 14 loaves of bread and 14 gallons of beer.

By the 17th century Flitwick manor house was being built, nicely situated close to the church, and among the interesting families who lived there were the Brooks who, through Mrs George Brooks, were linked to the Bruce family – the Earls of Elgin – of Ampthill. In the 19th century John Brooks was in touch with the famous St Joseph Paxton, of Crystal Palace fame, regarding specimens of *Musa Cavendishii.*

Flitwick spreads over a large area, cut in half by the railway which was partly responsible for its expansion. Eastwards lies the Moor, a wildlife site of great importance, and it was near here at Folly Farm that medicinal spring water was discovered by Henry Stevens in the 19th century, making Flitwick famous throughout Southern England, thanks to publicity through *The Lancet.* It lasted until the mid 1930s and then the land was returned to agricultural use.

It was around here in 1356 that 100 oxen had just been branded by Dunstable Priory men when a couple of desperadoes armed with bows and arrows stole them after chasing the terrified herders to nearly Ruxox Farm where they took refuge. This was a good place to choose as Ruxox had been a chapel of ease since 1150 when Philip de Sanvil gave it to Dunstable Priory. His son Gilbert strongly objected to the gift and ventured his spite on the chaplain. Later he contracted leprosy and, thinking it might be divine intervention, quickly made amends. Richard Dillingham of Flitwick must also have regretted his action when he stole from a house in Steppingley and got transported to Tasmania in 1832 as punishment. He fell on his feet as it happened and a letter in 1836 speaks of the good life he had found: 'I want for nothing in that respect. As for tea and sugar I could almost swim in it.'

Like many small rural communities Flitwick, meaning 'pasture by the Flitt', has completely changed within living memory, but records from the past exist to reflect upon, like a simple entry in the parish register for 1676 which reads, 'Thomas Pheasant who died for ye love of Mary Pierce'.

GRAVENHURST

Set in an agricultural area, east of Silsoe, this village has been a single parish since 1888 but physical differences still present an upper and lower part. Two churches were built here and the lower one knew its own age through an inscription by Sir Robert of Bilhemore in 1362 who rebuilt it. Also resting in peace in this ancient spot is Benjamin Pigott, 1606, who was supposed to be the first man in Bedfordshire to own a watch.

Upper Gravenhurst has its St Giles' church but was once just a chapelry of Shillington. It was said in 1549 that floodwater between these two villages was deep enough to drown people trying to get through. In more modern times some poachers were trying to get to Luton market with a load of plovers' eggs but knew their cart would be stopped and searched by men waiting for them so they hid their booty under the seats then kindly gave a grateful parson a lift to town knowing that nobody would stop him. Another time, the same family caused the parson great embarrassment when he called at their house unexpectedly with the Bishop who needed to wash his hands. The whole place was full of dead game, the proceeds of poaching the night before.

The Bedfordshire clanger, a suet pudding with meat at one end and jam the other, which gave a workman his dinner and sweet, had a new twist in Gravenhurst. The men ate everything except the meat which they took home for tomorrow's clanger, making the meat last a few days longer. Rural life could be particularly hard especially after a bad harvest. One farmer in this predicament called his eleven men together, who each earned eleven shillings, and told them one man had to go but, unanimously, they agreed to forego one shilling each for the eleventh man and solved the problem.

GREAT BARFORD

Mention this village and childhood memories return of picnics on soft grass in green meadows by a gentle river. Sometimes there were boats to see and always anglers to watch against a backdrop of pretty cottages, ancient inns and a 15th century parish church. This is just the riverside part of a fair sized village, east of Bedford, with the A1 a couple of miles away.

It was the building of Barford Bridge that made all the difference to the village. This sturdy structure of 17 pointed arches, once nicely described as 'simple in elegance', was built in accordance with the will of Sir Gerard Braybroke who died in 1429 and it certainly had an impact. By 1446 the burgesses of Bedford were appealing for a reduction in their rents due to loss of tolls and trade partly through the rival bridge.

Things got worse for in 1638 the river was made navigable by Arnold Spencer of Cople so that barges could get all the way from the east coast to Great Barford. Civil War and shortage of funds disrupted progress for some time then Arnold died and his two granddaughters inherited. The girls married two brothers from the Jemmatt family who carried on the business,

Great Barford

maintaining the waterway and collecting tolls.

In the late 1680s work progressed in getting barges to Bedford and the Quarter Sessions appointed their own man, Henry Ashley, to look after their interests. He quarrelled with the Jemmatt brothers, lost his temper and ended up in Great Barford with a pair of swords wanting to fight a duel. A court case was started to resolve the differences; this lasted nine years and was settled by one side having rights to traffic going upstream and the other to downstream traffic.

Another local dispute which ended in London came about after an 18th century election result gave only one vote difference between two candidates. So many accusations were made that the whole affair had to be settled in Westminster Hall. One of the witnesses was John Pedley, a local farmer and diarist, who unfortunately was also a hypochondriac. He suffered dreadfully in London, terrified he would catch smallpox from somebody there. At the end of the day he collected his six guineas expenses and by seven in the morning was in a post-chaise fleeing the city.

HARLINGTON

—— If you want magnificent views of the Chiltern Hills then you need to look no further than here. At the same time bide awhile at some crossroads in the heart of the village and see the 14th century church and several interesting and ancient timber-framed buildings. One of them is the Carpenter's Arms and outside stands a mounting block from the days when travellers needed to get back in the saddle after their beverage.

The railway arrived in 1868 and, at first, the station was called 'Harlington for Toddington', which partly explains why there is a Station Road in Toddington, some three miles away, but no station. By all accounts Harlington ran an efficient station for in 1934 it won the LMS Railway Shield.

It is through Bedfordshire's most famous son, John Bunyan, that Harlington is particularly well known. His arrest for preaching at nearby Lower Sampshill, interrogation by Squire Francis Wingate at Harlington House, now known as The Manor, and committal to Bedford for trial is well documented.

Supporting Squire Wingate in Bunyan's downfall was the rector of the parish church. Ironically a stained glass window depicting

The Pilgrim's Progress was eventually installed in the church and the altar is made from the wood of an oak tree where the poor tinker once preached. Another oak planted as a sapling by botanist Dr David Bellamy in 1988 thrives in place of the original.

HARROLD

This North Bedfordshire village is one of the county's most attractive. It is historical too, having been given by William the Conqueror to Judith his niece soon after 1066. It grew in importance because it had its own mill, for which the annual rent was 200 eels, and one of the few bridges over the Great Ouse. This is an unusual bridge, with narrow, curving lines and one of the arches is a 14th century example of Northamptonshire ironstone.

Had it not been for the obstinacy of two sisters, the Misses Trevor of Bromham, Harrold's beautiful bridge would have been demolished in 1847 and an iron one put in its place. This was the decision taken when the county prepared to take responsibility for the bridge away from the three proprietors who had previously paid for its upkeep. As well as the Misses Trevor, there was the Earl de Grey and the Alston family. It was decided the three should make a final contribution but the Trevor sisters immediately objected to being overcharged, although the other two agreed to pay. Arguments raged but the sisters would not be swayed from their conviction that they were being charged for two arches whereas they were only responsible for one. The authorities would not relent so eventually the whole idea was dropped – in the interests of posterity as it happened.

Harrold is probably best known to the visitor for its 18th century market house and its round lockup standing on the green. The uncomplimentary remark made by an official in 1811 that the market house was 'neither useful nor ornamental' seems to have been a minority view. Its 'butter' market comes from the word 'buttery' meaning food store or pantry. The village lockup was built in 1824 and is well preserved. It is round with a dunce's-cap roof and was used to restrain drunks and other sources of nuisance or as a temporary holding place for prisoners on the way to Bedford gaol. Apparently lockups were built round instead of square so the devil would have no corner to hide in to make the inmates any worse.

HAYNES

There are four 'ends' to Haynes, widely scattered between the A6 and the A600, but the conservation area covering Church End is particularly attractive. Here stand timber-framed houses, an ancient parish church and a Victorian coach-house leading to Haynes Park mansion, an imposing treasure, half a mile away. This was the manor of Hawnes, a name used for centuries from the Saxon 'Hegeness' meaning 'fences'. No doubt in days of open land, before the enclosure acts, fences were uncommon.

In the late 15th century the Brays obtained the manor and held it for a century. Then came the Newdigates, newcomers to the county, linked through marriage to the Conquest family at Houghton. Sir Roger Newdigate fell out with the local gentry who accused him of allowing his servant Ellis Rhys to beat up Thomas Percival of Haynes so severely only the intervention of two poor women saved his life. They also said he had conspired to free a rogue from Bedford gaol and generally not to co-operate with other justices. In turn he complained he had been assaulted and threatened on the queen's highway by the Earl of Kent and 30 of his riders from Wrest Park who said they would make it too hot at Haynes for him to stay. What irked the Earl of Kent as much as anything was that Sir Roger, who was the tax assessor, had deliberately undervalued Haynes and overcharged other

Haynes House

parishes to make up the loss. It seems the mansion in Haynes Park had been rebuilt so perhaps there was a need to be frugal. At least Newdigates found royal favour for James I and Queen Anne visited them in 1605, 1614 and 1619.

A well known Bedfordshire family, the Lukes, held the manor for a few years then sold it to Sir George Carteret, an ardent Royalist who had defended Jersey during the Civil War. He held out for the King to the end, at one time attacking Parliamentary ships like a pirate but finally, in 1651, he surrendered the island, and took refuge in France. He joined the French navy and was made a Vice-Admiral, but fortunes and politics change and, after some years, he was first imprisoned then banished from the country. Venice was his next stop where he stayed for three years and then came home at the restoration of Charles II and acquired high office for his loyalty. It was through lands he had been granted in America that we get the New Jersey of today.

The Carterets and their kin the Thynnes kept possession of Haynes Park from 1667 until 1914 when it was sold to become a boarding school for girls. In more recent years it was sold again after the school closed and remains to impress the passer-by.

HENLOW

Famous for its bow-stringers in days when the longbow reigned, this mid-Bedfordshire village is better known today for its RAF base and Henlow Grange Health Farm.

It is a large parish, as celebrations to mark Napoleon's exile to Elba in 1814 showed, when seating was provided for 500 people. Living at the Grange then was Thomas Alexander Raynsford who held two manors in Henlow and another in Langford. In 1820 his wife gave birth to a daughter, Matilda. Also being born in 1820, at Goldington, was Henry Addington, the son of a captain in the Royal Navy.

They met up in 1850 when Henry came to nearby Langford as vicar and they were married at Henlow parish church in 1852. A daughter was born in 1855 followed by twin girls in 1857 and then a son Thomas, in 1859. He was named after his grandfather who, unfortunately, never lived to see his grandchildren. It was his brother, Major General Raynsford, the last of seven sons belonging to old Richard Raynsford, who had taken over the

Grange and its estate by this time.

Well within living memory, Alan Lennox-Boyd came to the Grange. He was a well-known figure in mid-Bedfordshire which he represented as the Member of Parliament, eventually becoming Colonial Secretary.

 ## HIGHAM GOBION

—— The name appears on a signpost at the northern end of Barton-le-Clay and, for a time, the straight road runs along the edge of the village, on the right, passing fertile fields opposite. A few bends, as the road climbs fairly steeply, and we come to tiny Higham Gobion on our left. There is, firstly, expansive Manor Farm then St Margaret's church followed by the Old Rectory. Next, another house then it's on to nearby Shillington.

It is worth a pause though for this place is a bit of a mystery. Originally Higham, meaning 'high homestead', it was the Gobion family from Northampton who added their name to it. As early as 1202 Richard Gobion's name appears locally when he was a juror deliberating in the case of Ralf de Tivill against his tenant Gilbert who claimed his rent was a pound of pepper per year and not four shillings as Ralf insisted. Gilbert lost the case.

Perhaps in Highham Gobion's history there is a lesson for all workaholics. Dr Edmund Castell, a great 17th century scholar, came as rector to finish his huge *Lexicon Heptagloton*, a dictionary of several oriental languages which he started whilst Professor of Arabic at Cambridge. He drove himself relentlessly for over 17 years and spent every penny he had on the work. Sadly it was to no avail, few people wanted it. Many copies were destroyed by a fire and the rest were eaten by rats in a warehouse. His epitaph, which he wrote himself, is in Arabic and thought to be the earliest of its kind in the country. It says simply that he was buried here in the hope of a better place.

HOCKLIFFE

—— Straddling Watling Street and crossed by a road linking Woburn to Leighton Buzzard, Hockliffe has grown up with traffic and, in the early days, enjoyed the prosperity it brought, hence the large number of inns it supported to deal with the mass of coaches.

There was a downside too, the road also attracted unsavoury characters as labourer John Stokes discovered in 1670. He came home to find twenty shillings missing and some handkerchiefs. A neighbour said they had seen a young man close by wearing a brown periwig and blue stockings. John Stokes hurried southwards and found the thief in Markyate but, although he got the handkerchiefs back, his hard-earned money was all gone. To combat crime in the area the Hockliffe Union was formed in 1800 which brought together three other villages, Battlesden, Chalgrave and Tilsworth, in a joint venture.

Sometimes Hockliffe was called 'Hockley in the Hole', probably because of the frequently poor state of the main road. This was not surprising as originally tiny Battlesden and Hockliffe were responsible for maintaining two miles of road, which proved impossible. Later tollgates appeared and revenue was raised to meet maintenance costs, but fields had to be fenced off to stop drovers using them to bypass the tollgates.

Hockliffe got some unwelcome publicity in the 18th century when the rector, Dr William Dodd, was arrested for forgery. As the King's chaplain he had already had his royal appointment cancelled for trying to bribe the Lord Chancellor to get him the lucrative living of St George's. He was an excellent preacher and had several books published but could still not live within his means. He forged a bond in the name of the 5th Lord Chesterfield, a former pupil, but was caught, tried and sentenced to death. Great efforts were made to save him; even the great Dr Johnson petitioned on his behalf but clemency was not shown.

At Newgate prison he was put on public display for two hours before his execution to give the public a chance to see him at one shilling a head. At the gallows at Tyburn there was the biggest crowd ever assembled for a public execution. Rumours spread that he was going to be resuscitated afterwards by an undertaker in Goodge Street with the connivance of the hangman. As it happened he was left hanging long enough to prove otherwise.

HOUGHTON CONQUEST

—— Who would have thought the village of Houghton Conquest, just north of Ampthill, was once of sufficient importance to warrant two visits in the 17th century by the reigning monarch, James I.

Both these visits were as a guest of the Conquest family whose tenure as lords of the manor spread over five centuries. In the 13th century they added their name to the original 'Houghton' to distinguish if from the other Houghton near Dunstable and ensured that their name would remain long after the family was forgotten.

Their magnificent Tudor house called 'Conquest Bury' was demolished in the mid 1800s and prompted William Franklin of a well-known local family to pen: 'It has to time's resistless sway, With all its gable ends given way'. Fortunately it had earlier been captured on a watercolour by Thomas Fisher.

With the demise of the Conquests, and a few other notable families, the village declined until it was no longer a safe place to go after dark and people said 'Bedford gaol would fall when it did not contain a Houghton man'. Roads went unrepaired, church and school were neglected and crime was rife.

One of the reasons given for such a decline in moral standards was that there was no resident priest; they all preferred to live elsewhere, even one who held the position for 34 years. Upon his death in 1830 a bombshell descended on Houghton Conquest in the figure of the Reverend Thomas Barber. He was a strong, loudly spoken man, who carried a stick and was not afraid to use it. As a Justice of the Peace he sorted out the worst offenders in the village by having them transported and recovered monies owing to the church by certain landowners.

Gradually quality of life returned to Houghton Conquest to such a degree that in 1837, when the Reverend John Rose took over the now peaceful living, his brother-in-law John Burgon became such a constant visitor to the comfortable rectory and beautiful surroundings that he was invited to make it his home whenever he was away from Oxford and he did for 30 years.

HULCOTE AND SALFORD

The name of one means 'dwelling in a hollow' and the other 'willow-ford' and these two tiny villages have been a combined parish since 1933. They both had churches built, Hulcote's in 1593 and Salford's sometime in the 13th century.

Hulcote's ancient benefactor was Richard Chernock who grew up in the village after arriving with his family from Lancashire in 1541. When he became a man he 'reedified his parish church at his own proper charge and newe built his mansion house'. He was also sheriff of the county on three occasions and was father to 14 children, all included on his monument in St Nicholas' church in 1615. The Elizabethan church he left us is very special, being entirely from that period. His manor house did not survive beyond the early 1800s but his descendants who lived there became distinguished members of the county's squirearchy.

Salford is an older place – we read that the county's first coroner was Hugh de Salford who held the post in 1230 and timber being installed in St Mary's church then is still there today. Peter de Salford came later and was something of a character. He was appointed Sheriff on three occasions but in the first period, 1339, he got into debt to the Crown. His second term in office, in 1360, saw him thrown into prison for neglect of duty and he only seemed to get it right during his last term from 1361. He was also a Justice of the Peace which makes him one of the earliest on record in the county.

A Salford man who nearly went to gaol was Richard Lettins: he refused to pay Ship Money. This particular tax was most unpopular being imposed by King Charles I and opposed by parliament. Even so collectors were out in the shire counties and men were being sent to prison. They were not quick enough to catch Richard Lettins and all they could write on their defaulters' list was 'Gone to New England'.

St Mary's had a tower until 1867 when it was replaced by the present bellcote built to house three bells. Unfortunately one was stolen during repairs some years ago.

HUSBORNE CRAWLEY

—— At the heart of this village is a conservation area covering the ancient church, several timber-framed cottages and an old manor farmhouse. They huddle together around a triangular green and create a picture postcard scene.

There have been some interesting characters living here, as monuments in the church confirm, and one of them was Talbot Williamson, lord of the manor in the 18th century. He took a keen interest in the village though he preferred to live in London for much of the year, being at the court of George III.

We find that Talbot was a kindly man, well educated with an interest in the classics and a love for the flute. He was quite protective of his brother Edward, vicar of Millbrook, and regularly sent him delicacies from London, such as oysters, lobsters and melons and once even a nice new wig and some soap. In return Edmund sent him hares, partridges and mince pies via the Dunstable coach.

Some good quality estate houses were built along the road to Woburn and the village also benefited in 1867 under the Duke of Bedford's school-building programme. Fifty-four children were admitted of whom only nine could read at all. The teacher had a mammoth task and probably found, as Charlotte Young described in *The Daisy Chain*, that 'classroom stillness was irksome to such wild colts'.

KEMPSTON

—— This is a spreading town that joins onto Bedford like a suburb but in fact is one of our oldest places, originally called 'Caembes'. There are plenty of 'Ends' here, some way out, like West End or Box End, others closer like Green End or Church End, where All Saints was built in the 12th century to be at the centre of its hamlets in a pleasant spot near the river.

The King William inn is a landmark in the High Street; its handsome black and white exterior is from the 17th century, though other parts are older. It takes us back to a time when Kempston was still a village, with rural problems which included poaching, to which men were sometimes driven by need. For example, when two brothers named Lilley were apprehended, one explained that although he worked from light to dark he was only paid seven shillings and could not maintain his pregnant wife and two children. Unfortunately the brothers injured a keeper and that cost them their lives.

Under the Saxon Centre there was once the largest Anglo Saxon cemetery in the county and many finds between 1850 and 1888 are credited to a curate of All Saints, the Reverend Samuel Fitch, and James Wyatt, a well-known local archaeologist. Just down the road in 1875, Kempston Barracks was being built at a cost of £50,000 leaving us with the imposing red brick Keep of today. It housed the Bedford Regiment, raised as the 16th Foot in 1688, which was already holding several battle honours including Blenheim, under the Duke of Marlborough, where the soldiers were at the forefront of the action and suffered badly.

The Bedfords were in the Boer War in 1901, commemorated by a statue near Bedford Bridge, and in the First World War were in action from the start as part of the Old Contemptibles that stopped the great German advance when it seemed nothing could. In 1919 they amalgamated with the Hertfordshires, through a long military association, and became the Beds and Herts, one of the finest county regiments. In the Second World War they fought at Dunkirk, in North Africa and Italy and against the Japanese in Burma where they wreaked havoc behind the enemy lines in the jungles and earned the distinction of destroying the largest supply depot in the campaign. Opposite the Keep a rightly impressive memorial records the sacrifices made by the regiment which now forms part of the Royal Anglian Regiment.

KENSWORTH

——— High on the downs above Watling Street, and close to Whipsnade, this parish belonged to Hertfordshire until 1897 when it was exchanged for Markyate. Wells had to be dug so deep that water was drawn by donkey-wheel and one of these ingenious contraptions, from Bury Park Farm, went to Luton Museum.

Kensworth's elevated position allowed for a signalling device to be built during the Napoleonic Wars, lined up to the next one at Lilley, to give warning of an invasion. It seems it was pulled down – rather prematurely perhaps – in 1814 when we were celebrating Napoleon's exile to Elba.

There has been a parish church at Kensworth since Norman times, with alterations and renovations down the ages, like the fine tower with its prominent stair-turret from the 15th century. In 1694 St Mary's suffered disruption from 65 members of the congregation led by Luton ironmonger Thomas Marsom, when they 'broke the peace of the church'. They went on to form Baptist meetings in Luton. There was a more sinister disturbance to the peace of the church in the early 19th century when corpses were required for dissection. Having buried his wife on Saturday, a distraught husband returned at an early hour to mourn at her graveside only to find her body lying on top, ready for the cart. It was many years before the authorities curbed this evil trade.

KEYSOE

Called 'Caysoo' before 1749, this village in the north of the county has an unusual ghost story attached to it. It seems a vicar discovered his wife was having an affair so he killed the man in a duel. Some people say the lover's ghost appears every year on the anniversary of his death.

Another strange event from Keysoe was the miracle cure of devout Anne Freeman on 14th April 1910. She had been an invalid for 16 years and had been seen by 24 doctors. Deterioration had come after rheumatic fever and pleurisy left her lower body 'cold, limp and lifeless'. Then she had a vision and heard a voice from heaven, 'Daughter, arise and go to work in my vineyard', and she described what she felt as an electric shock. Health and vigour flooded back and she left her sickbed immediately.

What could also be described as miraculous, or near to it, was William Dicken's fall from the church tower in 1718. He had been pointing the steeple when he slipped, hitting the battlements on top of the tower first, which broke his leg and foot, then tumbling down to the ground. He survived the fall and his story is told on a plaque, which lists rather too many things he supposedly said on his way down. The lofty tower of St Mary's church is a high point in the county.

Keysoe was also where our last working post-mill stood, sadly destroyed by a storm in 1946, but what does remain in our minds are the words of wisdom from the old thatched Baptist chapel:

A friendly word
A kindly smile
A helpful act
And life's worthwhile.

Keysoe Row in 1989

KNOTTING

—— Close to the Northamptonshire border, this tiny village must be one of the smallest in the county and has a small-sized church to suit. It was here on the Shrove Tuesdays of 1634 to 1636 that cock-fighting took place in the chancel with the vicar and his churchwardens involved. It caused such an outcry that in 1637 chancel gates were installed, to be kept locked at all times except during a service.

St Margaret's flat-topped tower was built in 1615 but the church is much older and there is the base of a preaching cross in the graveyard that is medieval. The church was rebuilt in the 13th century and lord of the manor in 1247 was John Buszard who was in dispute with nine local men and one woman who wanted to graze livestock on land that belonged to him. The issue was resolved by agreement that – in return for limited grazing rights – each of them would give him two chickens at Christmas, two dozen eggs at Easter and six days labour throughout the year.

By the mid 1700s the manor was held by Henry Pye whose son, Henry James Pye, succeeded then sold the manor to the Duke of Bedford in 1774, keeping the advowson of St Margaret's and of nearby Souldrop's church. Henry became a Member of Parliament for Berkshire, at the same time publishing several poems and topical odes he had written. His lack of talent resulted in many uncomplimentary comments especially from his political opponents. In 1790 the celebrated Poet Laureate Thomas Wharton died and Henry was given the honour of replacing him, for political reasons, and he became the butt of jokes and ridicule from contemporary critics from then on.

The Duke of Bedford sold Knotting in 1884 but left a fine legacy by way of the village school.

LEIGHTON BUZZARD

—— Close to the border with Buckinghamshire, in the south-west of the county, the old market town of Leighton Buzzard enjoys a rural situation yet remains easily accessible. Leisure pursuits might include rambling in 74 acres of beautiful grassland at Stockgrove, the county's first country park, or cruising on the Grand Union Canal which runs through neighbouring Linslade. Until 1965 Linslade and Leighton Buzzard were separate but they amalgamated and Leighton Linslade Urban District Council was formed, which later became part of South Bedfordshire District.

The canal was opened in 1805 as the Grand Junction Canal, linking London with the Midlands and it was a boon, particularly to the sand quarrying concerns, for the barges could carry very heavy loads, cheaply, over long distances. Ironically, it was the canal that prevented Leighton Buzzard getting a railway station when this more efficient transport system was put to the vote at a public meeting in 1831. The scheme was opposed, through fear of competition, so the railway station for Leighton Buzzard was built at Linslade instead.

Coaches brought trade to Leighton Buzzard in the 19th century and the impressive Swan Hotel in the High Street, with its Georgian façade and imposing entrance, was a coaching stop on the Oxford to Cambridge run. There was also a coach to London every day that left from an inn with the unusual name of the Eagle and Child which once stood in the Market Square. The Swan was where twenty local men belonging to the Civil Society used to meet in the 18th century to talk and enjoy the beer. But if attendance was low for any reason they felt obliged to switch to wine or punch to make up the difference for the landlord so absenteeism was not appreciated.

Opposite the Swan is Leighton Buzzard's famous Market Cross which has looked down the High Street since the early 15th century. For many years this was where the banns of marriage were published and, in 1751, it was put to a more sinister use when two poor women stood there being denounced as witches. Their accusers were unable to use the traditional method of submersing them in water because the river Ouzel was too shallow at the time, which probably saved their lives. This unusual pentagonal structure, with five carved figures on the upper of two tiers, has needed a fair amount of restoration over the centuries. It was once surrounded by iron railings but they were never very popular.

The oldest building in Leighton Buzzard is the cathedral-like church of All Saints which was started in 1277. It is the third largest church in the county and at 191 feet its spire is amongst the loftiest of landmarks. There are fine stained glass windows by Kemp, who could not become a priest because of a bad

The Market Cross, Leighton Buzzard, in 1964

stammer yet left an even greater gift for posterity. A walk round reveals medieval graffiti and some misericords from the 14th century plus a magnificent eagle lectern carved in oak made especially for All Saints and believed to be one of oldest of its type in the country. The font, where countless babies have been blessed since it was first fashioned out of local limestone, is even older than the church. Just outside is a very special war memorial, a 20 ton block of granite believed to be the largest ever quarried in England. It complements the attractive Church Square from where a lane leads to a recreation ground and a bandstand which is a reminder of the Festival of Britain, giving children a place to play close to the town centre.

Markets have played an important part in Leighton Buzzard. Fairs were held every February and brought hundreds of horses, cattle and sheep crowding through the streets to be sold. Some residents hired out tethering places in front of their houses to the horse traders; others, including the bank next to the Swan Hotel, put up temporary post and chains along the pavement to keep the livestock away. This bank was the first in Leighton Buzzard and was built in 1866 by John-Dillon Basset, son of the founder, a former draper and well-known Quaker. An example of Victorian confidence, this imposing building was designed by Alfred Waterhouse, the same architect who later produced plans for Shire Hall in Bedford.

LIDLINGTON

A steep hill leading to the busy A507 acts as a backdrop to this mid-Beds village which at the Domesday survey was held by the Abbess of Barkway. It turns up in the records again in 1247 when the Abbess erects gallows in the parish to deal with the lawless and, by doing so, breaks the law herself.

A real character with a Lidlington connection was Brackley Kennett who became Lord Mayor of London in 1779. His journey to fame and fortune was via the wine trade and he worked for a time as a wine waiter. It was said of him by way of ridicule, once he was in high office, 'that you only had to ring a bell and Kennett would appear'. Whether this influenced him into taking no part to quell the terrible riots in the City during 1780 is speculative but he failed to do his duty and was arrested.

At a special trial he was charged with 'wilful misconduct and neglect of duty' but since the first part of the charge could not be proven he walked free though not from public scorn and contempt.

Like many ancient manors, Lidlington changed hands numerous times until, early in the 19th century, it became part of the Woburn Estate. This was to prove providential for the parish church which had troubles even after its rebuilding in 1809.

One of the problems was that it had been built only large enough for the existing congregation. When a much better preacher arrived a chancel and gallery had to be added to cope with the overflow. But by 1886 it seemed the building was in danger of collapse and slowly slipping down its hillside site, just as, in 1708, the original tower had leaned like Pisa. A new church was needed.

Everyone knew the 9th Duke of Bedford was a generous man but he had already offered to build a new school, which, incredibly, the village elders turned down. Later they tried to change their minds but to no avail. Fortunately there was no dissent when he offered to build a new church, at his own expense, and this is the fine sandstone building we see today gracing the centre of Lidlington.

LITTLE STAUGHTON

—— Up to the 20th century this north Bedfordshire village had survived its normal trials and tribulations like any other ancient village. The church of St Margaret was dominant – and prominent too with its tall spire pointing to the sky. Attendance was compulsory and excommunication possible as Agnes Halle found out in 1599 after 'being utterly undone with trying to bring up a child her seducer had left her with'.

Everything changed for Little Staughton in 1942; the war took men away and then the Baptist chapel was demolished together with some 20 houses and a couple of pubs. An airfield was needed and half the village stood in the way. The Americans came and used the base as a depot for maintenance and repair of B17 bombers. Badly damaged planes, limping home from a raid, would try to put down at Little Staughton instead of their home base and sometimes failed to reach the runway.

The RAF took over the airfield on 1st March 1944 and it became an operational station for the elite 582 Lancaster squadron and Mosquitos of 109 Squadron, both engaged in crucial but hazardous pathfinder duties. These involved arriving over the target first and then directing approaching bombers to the right spot. It was so dangerous that Air Vice Marshall Bennett of the pathfinders predicted that if any of his men were awarded a Victoria Cross it would be posthumously, and so it proved to be.

Two pilots from Little Staughton were awarded this highest honour after an action in which they lost their lives, one from

St Margaret's church, Little Staughton

each squadron. The first was Acting Squadron Leader Robert Palmer DFC and the other was Major Edwin Swales DFC, a South African officer. Little remains from those anxious times though the parish church, now All Saints, does have a memorial to remind us of the deeds of brave men and a new Baptist chapel was built in the village centre some years after the war.

LUTON

This is the county's giant, the supplier of employment and provider of education for so many people that it is no wonder there is an affinity. It started a long time ago when Luton was the centre of the hat trade and straw plait became a cottage industry in the villages – with children at plait schools (see Clifton, for example) learning that money came first.

Close to the retail heart of the town stands St Mary's, the parish church. When it was first built in the 13th century, Luton was village size, but the church grew as the parish did. It was enlarged in the 14th century and changes were made in the 15th century. The result is that Luton has one of the largest parish churches in the land, and one that is very impressive. It was built in a chequerboard pattern using flint and limestone up to its many battlements. Inside is just as spectacular. Several figures from Luton's historical past repose here including the Wenlocks, whose monument makes a very bold statement. One of these became Lord John Wenlock of Someries, the name of the old castle he had started to rebuild in red brick. Unfortunately he lived during the War of the Roses, changed sides twice and was killed just as it seemed he had a third change of mind. Other notables in St Mary's include the Rotherhams, Crawleys, Hoos and Acworths, familiar names in the town.

The spread of the Luton area from Hyde to Leagrave and Stopsley to the Dunstable border came about through the magnet of employment but, incredibly, the town dragged its feet when railways came. Some objected to using the Great Moor for the purpose and so by 1858 all Luton got was a branch line to Dunstable to connect with the London to Birmingham route. This was soon seen as a disadvantage and, fortunately, the line from Bedford to London, which had gone through Hitchin instead, had become seriously overcrowded. It was proposed that the Midland Railway construct a line from Bedford, through Luton, and on to London, and it was welcomed. The Great Moor was used but in exchange the community received People's Park, Pope's Meadow and Bell's Close. In 1904 the town also acquired Wardown Park, vastly extending its leisure acres. In the meantime it was believed 3,000 navvies would eventually arrive to build the new line and there was worry over security. The town had one day constable and two nightwatchmen and it was felt that at least communications would improve if the superintendent in charge could have a horse.

The hat trade was healthy at this time and straw plait was booming. In 1869, at the time the Corn Exchange was erected in Park Street, plait halls were also built. These were in Cheapside and Waller Street so the business need no longer be conducted in George Street, in all weathers. Afterwards manufacturers gave a tea party in the Corn Exchange for 1,200 female workers.

Shortly before the First World War, engineering manufacturing arrived and the hat trade started to decline. These new factories geared up for war work and soon girls as well as men were working in munitions. The house in Wardown Park became a convalescent home for wounded soldiers, some convinced they had seen a ghostly housekeeper roaming around. This beautiful Victorian house, with its impressive carriage porch bearing terracotta busts of leading figures, like Disraeli and Dickens, was built in 1875. It was the home of a solicitor before passing to Luton with the park and, from 1931, becoming a museum. Immediately after the peace declaration of June 1919 there was a riot in the town involving many troops which got out of hand and the Town Hall was burned down, unfortunately with numerous treasured records, but a new and better one was built and lessons were learned. Wardown Park received a field gun and an army tank, which were kept on display until taken away for scrap in World War II together with the park's railings.

As the hat trade was replaced by companies which became household names like Skefco, Bagshaw, George Kent, Commer Cars and Vauxhall, Luton became the place of opportunity in engineering for most of the 20th century. From the small aerodrome of 1938 where private planes taxied along the grass, Luton Airport emerged in the 1960s to give the county another means of travel and later a modernised town centre introduced a new form of shopping, all under one roof.

In 1947, hot from a Luton press, there first appeared a gem of a publication called the *Bedfordshire Magazine* which was the brainchild of the founder, Harold White. He launched the magazine in the interest of furthering knowledge of the county where he was born and raised. Harold White started as a junior with the *Luton News*, straight from Luton Modern School, and was paid ten shillings a week. In due course he became a director of the Leagrave Press and then launched his own company, the well-known White Crescent Press in Crescent Road. In his spare time he was secretary of the Bedfordshire Historical Record Society and his love of the written word resulted in a long friendship with George Bernard Shaw. Harold published the last work of the famous writer and then was pleased to receive five years' subscription for *Bedfordshire Magazine* from him, even though the elderly genius was 92 at the time.

Bedfordshire Magazine ran for about 40 years and is a compendium of county knowledge that will ensure the work of Harold White will be long remembered and appreciated.

MARSTON MORETAINE

——— Orange-coloured lorries bearing the name 'Marston Valley Brick Company' were once a common sight here but all that has changed. A bypass speeds traffic away from the village and a huge tree-planting programme is well under way in Marston Vale.

But some things never change, like the second look you have to give the parish church of St Mary whose tower is completely detached. If only some giant hand could pick it up and put it back where it belonged our sense of order would be restored, but this would mean it was no longer one of only three dozen of its type in the country.

What influenced our 14th century ancestors at the time is not recorded but perhaps a clue lies in the lowest part of the tower, which is older than the rest, and has a single arched opening so high up it could only be reached by a long ladder. This, together with walls six feet thick and its own well, indicates that it was a place of refuge originally – but from what?

Too late as a defence against the Danes, the doorway was also too high for even the worst floods so could it have been an escape from the plague? It has long been thought that the village, which lies to the north of the church, was in the south before being devastated by a 'visitation' of the plague. It fits the bill but, alas, we shall never know the secret of the tower.

The village legend is much more colourful: it seem the tower was built next to the church but the devil himself picked it up and moved it. Being so heavy he could only manage 70 feet and gave up. Later he sat in its single doorway looking southward and from here he noticed the owner of a field playing leap-frog over a large stone instead of being in church.

This stone, which is still there, deeply embedded in the ground, is called 'Devil's Jumps' because that's what the devil did – he leapt from the tower onto the stone, grabbed the hapless landowner and sprang back to Hell with him. The area where this all happened became known as 'The Jumps' and there was once an inn there by the same name.

No doubt this story has been used as a warning to non-attenders of St Mary's, which is a massive church even without its tower. Prominent amongst past dignitaries whose lives are commemorated inside are the Moretyenes, who gave the village its double-barrelled name and built the church, also the Snagge family members who once resided in the beautiful 16th century moated manor house, one of the village landmarks. A descendant of this family was John Snagge, a famous radio commentator on the BBC often covering the Oxford v Cambridge Boat Race.

It was Sarah, Dowager Duchess of Marlborough, who bought the Snagge's old manor and she was a most bad-tempered old lady by all accounts. It has been said she once blackened the face of a granddaughter's portrait and wrote underneath 'She is much blacker within'. When she died in 1744 at 84 her vast property went to Earl Spencer who sold up in due course and went to Althorp.

MAULDEN

The name of this widespread village means 'cross-on-a-hill' and as that must refer to St Mary's church it is appropriate, for this landmark of Maulden can be plainly seen for miles. A footpath down the hill leads to a cluster of ancient cottages and the old George pub whilst the road from the church passes a fine school built in 1880 by the Duke of Bedford.

In earlier days, Earls of Ailsbury from Houghton House, Ampthill were lords of the manor and there is a mausoleum behind the church where members of this family were laid to rest. One of them, Robert, who died in 1685, had a coffin made of lead placed inside another one made of wood which must have been quite a struggle for the pall bearers getting it up the hill and into the crypt. Soon after the funeral 32 members of the household learned they were to receive a small legacy from the Earl.

The family were understandably popular which was the undoing of the next Earl of Ailsbury. Being a James II supporter, by an oath of loyalty, he got thrown into the Tower of London by King William and stayed there for nearly a year. Lady Ailsbury was allowed visits and, on one of them, got pregnant. She died in childbirth and her prematurely born daughter only survived her for 18 months. Apparently nobody ever saw the baby smile during her short life because, it was said, she had been 'conceived in melancholy'.

Soon the Earl was released and tried to quietly make his way home, just pausing at Maulden church to pay respects to his late wife. But the word was out, bells rang and the streets were lined with cheering crowds. The King was furious at this show of support for a man who, having fallen from grace, could no longer be Lord Lieutenant of the county yet was still able to command so much affection. Not long after this incident the Earl 'elected' to go into exile in Belgium, leaving the district and 'that beautiful habitation that I doted on', never to return.

There has been a church at Maulden, in one form or another, since the 12th century. Many changes have occurred over the centuries to church and village alike but the continuity remains. It is well worth the climb to St Mary's, even though the village boundaries are too distant to be seen. That to the east stretches as far as Clophill cross-roads and, to the west, the top of Oaklands Hill, just before Ampthill. It was here, just in Maulden, that William Claridge, an Ampthill grocer in Victorian times, built the elegant Hill House which, because of his profession, became known by the locals as the 'lard and treacle villa'.

MELCHBOURNE

——— The early history of this village, some 12 miles north of Bedford shows that by 1264 a market and a fair had been granted to the lord. The Knights Hospitallers were also here, building their preceptory 'a right fair place of squared stone' after the Crusades. It was dissolved in 1538 and, by 1550, belonging to John Russell, the newly created Earl of Bedford.

Perhaps being so remote from Woburn was the reason

Edward, the 3rd Earl of Bedford, sold it in 1608 to the well-respected Lord St John of Bletsoe. It was too dilapidated to rebuild so it was demolished and a new one built in its place. In 1741 Melchbourne House was considerably enlarged and the family had acquired another title – Earl of Bolingbroke. As well as a large park, there were extensive gardens attached where greenhouses and conservatories were erected.

In the 19th century, the St Johns built a new school (now a private house) to replace the old Sunday school of 1787. In the early 1900s the Scout movement got underway and in 1910 Lord St John became the first County President. Melchbourne Park changed hands in 1934 and, in due course, the mansion became desirable apartments.

MEPPERSHALL

An agricultural village south of Shefford, Meppershall is off the beaten track, peaceful and quiet. It possesses an impressive timber-framed manor house from the early 17th century and a parish church, mainly 15th century. It also has a place called 'The Hills', which is a clue to a time when Meppershall was anything but peaceful.

On this site stood a motte and bailey castle, the home of William de Meppershall, who was the royal larderer to Henry I. Unfortunately Henry's son and heir drowned crossing the Channel, which left his sister Matilda heir to the throne. When the time came the barons rejected her and chose her cousin Stephen instead. Meppershall got involved in the squabble that followed because William de Meppershall supported Matilda so his castle was attacked by Stephen, with ordinary people getting caught up in the siege.

There is a sequel to this story that left Meppershall with another memento of royal intrigue. Matilda, as we know, did a deal with Stephen, agreeing he should rule providing her son followed as Henry II. This was done, but then Thomas à Becket was murdered in 1170 by the King's men which so disgusted the population, that chapels of remembrance appeared, including St Thomas the Martyr at Meppershall, south of the village, run by Chicksands Priory. Next door is Chapel Farm and the old chapel was put to good use eventually as a barn.

An oddity over parish boundaries in the 19th century meant that a part of Meppershall belonged to Hertfordshire. The boundary was believed to go through the dining room of the rectory and a beam carried the advice: 'If you wish to go to Hertfordshire, hitch a little nearer the fire'.

MILLBROOK

—— This village was ancient even before Henry VIII confined Catherine of Aragon to his nearby castle whilst he got on with his divorce at Dunstable. It was an aptly named village until the old mill was demolished.

Just west of Ampthill, on the A507, the road into Millbrook drops steeply away on the right, between wooded hills and high ground, twisting and turning over traffic-calming humps. At one point the road is so low and gloomy it has been considered either the 'Valley of the Shadow of Death' in John Bunyan's *The Pilgrim's Progress* or his 'Slough of Despond' but village beliefs have been proved wrong from time to time. One of these concerned noises parishioners said were coming from the statues of Sir William and Mary Heuett in 1864 after their effigies were moved from their Elizabethan resting place.

The rector tried to solve the problem by putting the couple in the rectory cellar but the strange whip-like sound in the church continued. Believing a burial in consecrated ground in the churchyard was the best solution the rector had this done but to no avail. It was not until the roof of the nave fell in some years later that the reason for the cracking became apparent.

Years later a team of enthusiasts got to work with spades to recover the figures but they had been badly interred and damage was severe. The knight's head was missing altogether because it had been found by a man digging in the graveyard and taken home. Eventually it was restored so, hopefully, the souls of these much disturbed people now rest in peace.

A Millbrook congregation had been described in 1766 by the great preacher John Wesley as 'plain serious people' but some got very roused in 1835 over the new Poor Law Act of 1834, especially as unemployment was rife at the time. With coal at 2/6d per ton, which they could not afford, they were further incensed when John Chapman and Ann Wheeler of Millbrook were sent to prison for a month for picking up sticks in a field. Law and order broke down in the district and there were riots which led to an investigation by a select committee of the House of Commons.

The population of Millbrook was much greater then. It became one of the Duke of Bedford's estate villages in the 19th century and it reflects this period. Modern times have brought a golf course, equestrian centre and a vehicle-proving ground but the welcoming Chequers pub belongs to earlier days.

A curious little note at the end of our tale comes from the journal of Cecilia Parke, writing from Park House in 1839: 'there was great festivities at Christmas when the schoolchildren of Ampthill and Millbrook had their tree all lighted up'. This was before Prince Albert had even married Queen Victoria let alone 'introduced' the Christmas tree into this country.

MILTON BRYAN

—— Close to the southern edge of Woburn Park lies the tiny village of Milton Bryan, birthplace in 1801 of Sir Joseph Paxton, one of Bedfordshire's remarkable men, who started life as a waif after his father died which prompted him to tell his children that they would never know how nourishing a turnip was until they had to live on it.

Joseph was befriended in Essex by a Quaker family who gave him board for work and some education. Eventually he returned to Milton Bryan and got a job as a gardener's boy on Sir Gregory Page-Turner's estate at nearby Battlesden Park within walking distance. By the time he was 20, Joseph 'increased' his age by two years and was taken on at the Horticultural Society at Chiswick. His natural ability was noticed by the 6th Duke of Devonshire who offered him the job of head gardener at Chatsworth House.

The Duke gave Joseph a free hand which resulted in many notable enterprises such as the Great Conservatory which Queen Victoria once drove through in a carriage to see the tropical plants, the Emperor Fountain to honour the Tsar and the Lily House where Joseph nurtured small South American lilies from Kew, which grew until they were four and a half feet across. The public flocked to Chatsworth to see Joseph's daughter sitting on a floating leaf.

Milton Bryan in 1981

When the Great Exhibition of 1851 was planned to encourage trade and industries of all nations Joseph sent in a design for a building that could be completed in nine months, with a feasible removal afterwards, just as the requirements stipulated. It was accepted out of 240 entries.

Joseph used the same method of construction he had employed on the Chatsworth Lily House, but on a massive scale. Nothing had been seen like it before: a third of a mile long and wider than a football pitch, the country watched and waited as the huge building took shape. The railway delivered 200 miles of sash bars, 25 miles of guttering and a million square feet of glass. All sections were interchangeable and it went up like a giant Meccano set – in just six months.

Quite a few exhibits came from Bedfordshire, like the Howard plough made at the Britannia Works in Bedford and as Dunstable and Luton were famous for their straw hats these were displayed in various stages of manufacture. At the end of the Great Exhibition, which was a huge commercial success, Joseph received £7,000 and a knighthood. He moved the building to Sydenham and there it was redesigned and rebuilt to become one of the wonders of the world.

At this time Joseph was commissioned by Baron Meyer Rothschild to build Mentmore Towers near Leighton Buzzard. It was a mammoth task spread over five years and was innovative in many respects. George Stokes, an architect, had married into the Paxton family and assisted in the work. The Rothschild family commissioned two more 'Paxton' designed houses, one near Paris and the other at Geneva. Then Sir Edward Page-Turner engaged him to build him a new mansion in the French chateau style at Battlesden Park. It seemed Joseph's life had gone full circle. He had left Bedfordshire as a gardener and was now back as a famous architect, but this was his last assignment. He died in 1865 and his wife Sarah had a stained glass window put into St Peter's church at Milton Bryan in his honour.

MILTON ERNEST

Some interesting characters have been associated with this village, which is on the A6 north of Bedford and close to a loop in the Great Ouse. One of these was Thomas Rolt, whose family name appears in many Bedfordshire parishes, and first occurs in Milton Ernest in 1542. He started acquiring land and by 1573 also held a manor.

Following this line of descent we arrive at Thomas Rolt the fourth, who, in loving memory of his wife Susanna and acting on her instructions, installed an unusual 'bread box' in the parish church in 1729. This is a neat, wall-mounted container with spaces for twelve 'two-penny loaves', a weekly gift to the poor, but not 'for ever' as Susanna had willed.

Thomas also made a contribution to the lovely old church of All Saints by donating a huge brass chandelier which hung from its long chain for the next two centuries. Unfortunately the chain broke and the chandelier came crashing down, smashing itself to pieces on the floor. It was thought to be beyond repair but the British Oxygen Company considered otherwise and painstakingly put the whole thing back together again.

In the early 18th century a young married couple arrived at the village direct from London where the young man, Underhill Robinson, had recently finished his apprenticeship as a printer. He set up his printing press and his first job was a book by the Reverend John Hunt of Newport Pagnell called *Evangelical - Sanctification Truly Stated and Vindicated*. It was most unusual to find a printing press outside London let alone deep in the countryside. People must have wondered, why Milton Ernest?

As it happened the young printer was born in the county. His father had been the vicar of Colmworth but died suddenly so he had been fixed up with an apprenticeship in London. The book he printed was the first in the county – there was not another printing press until 1766, some 47 years later. Unfortunately it was Underhill Robinson's first and last job: he died shortly afterwards at only 27 and was buried in All Saints.

In the next century, William Butterfield came to the village and restored the parish church. He also built Milton Hall, the bold Victorian landmark that has been put to many uses over the years.

NORTHILL

As if designed to please, Northill projects all the characteristic charm of an English village. It has ancient dwellings and a nice old pub, a village green and a pond, all overlooked by a handsome parish church. Not far away, in its own setting, is the Grange, a substantial building from about 1700.

St Mary's church, large and lofty, dates from the 14th century and was made collegiate in 1404 by Henry IV with a rector and four fellows. Traces of those college days show up in local place names such as College Wood and College Meadow.

Northill is noted by family researchers for its collection of parish registers and the churchwarden accounts are also very revealing. In 1563, for example, they were levying the 'Lincoln Farthing' – a farthing charge on the house of anybody who had not made the pilgrimage to Lincoln Cathedral to join the Whitsuntide procession. They also provided Morris dancers with bells, coats and shoes and then the energetic troupe would visit other parishes with their ancient dance routine, bringing good luck and, in return, collecting for the church fund.

One of the hamlets attached to Northill is Ickwell, well known for its large village green, colourwashed cottages and a lofty maypole that has heralded the coming of May Day for centuries. It was the birthplace of one of Bedfordshire's most famous sons, Thomas Tompion, the 'Father of English Watchmaking', who made the world's first balance-spring from a design by his friend Robert Hooke of the Royal Society. From his premises off Fleet

Ickwell Green near Northill surrounds a common grazing ground

Street, Thomas became watchmaker to kings and his fame as the best craftsman in London spread to the Continent – and it all started at his father's blacksmith's shop on Ickwell Green where he made agricultural tools.

Although by 1664 Thomas was already 25 he left the parish to become apprenticed to a London clock-maker. Perhaps it was no coincidence that, at the same time, John Oliver from London was skilfully fashioning heraldic windows at St Mary's where Thomas's father was a churchwarden. Thomas Tompion never married; he devoted his life to his craft and earned a place amongst the famous in Westminster Abbey. There is a Tompion memorial plaque in St Mary's and it is claimed that the church clock, and another one installed on the stable block at Ickwell Bury, were both products of 'the local boy made good'.

OAKLEY

Oakley, north-west of Bedford, grew up by the side of the river and one stretch of the water must have been known as Stafford for we read, in 1227, that 'Richard de Pabeham fell from a certain mare into the water of Stafford so that he died'. A bridge was built sometime before 1505 for that was when the first record of Stafford Bridge appears.

Maintenance was an expensive business; the county had taken responsibility for causeways from the early 17th century but not bridges, which were usually paid for by local landowners. One of them was the 4th Duke of Bedford, who came to Oakley in 1737 following his purchase of the Levinz estate from the descendants of Judge Sir Creswell Levinz, a former Attorney General. A hunting lodge was included and, in due course, this received the expert attention of Henry Holland who was architect to the Prince of Wales and responsible for Carlton House and the original Brighton Pavilion. He married 'Capability' Brown's daughter, Bridget, and the men frequently worked together. Oakley House became a delightful home for other members of the Russell family to enjoy.

Lord and Lady Ampthill came to Oakley House in 1918 moving from Milton Ernest where they had lived since their marriage in 1894. Their two children, Leo, 16, and his sister Phyliss, two years younger, must have approved of their new home for they decided to make a scale model in their free time. It was a daunting task getting all the measurements right and then, whilst the village carpenter, Arthur Jones, made the shell to their design, they bought themselves a fretwork saw by Hobbies Limited that worked on a treadle.

Painstakingly copying all the furniture and decor in the house they made each piece to scale, even the tiny brass stair-rods, and methodically over the years their creation grew into a masterpiece of youthful endeavour. Eventually it was shown at the Victoria and Albert Museum of Childhood, and, after that, at the Cecil Higgins Museum in Bedford.

ODELL

When Walter de Wahulls built his castle here he must have noticed the beautiful view his defensive position afforded him. The castle has gone but the view endures of a winding river in its rural setting. Walter was a Flemish adventurer who had joined the Normans in their conquest and 'Wahul' meaning 'woad hill' became 'Odell'. The Wahulls were not very prosperous, even after a market started in 1221 brought extra revenue; John in 1336 was holding only Langford in addition to Odell.

We read that the leather industry, which developed in neighbouring Harrold from the 19th century, started in Odell when Edward Rate arrived from Wales. He was a fellmonger, or hide dealer, and knew tanning. Providentially he met a Londoner who could finish and dye, so they went into business in Horsefair Lane. Then Edward quarrelled with the landlord so they moved to Harrold and prospered there. Unfortunately, at 75, Edward fell into one of his own pits full of foul tanning matter and died.

Back in 1635, London lawyer William Alston had built a house on the site of the old castle and bought the estate. A lot of the history of the village has been entwined with this family who remained until comparatively recent times. In contrast to the sober Peter Bulkeley, one of the Alstons sons, Vere John, who became the vicar, got so merry one night he fell off his horse. This surprised him as he claimed he had only drunk two bottles of wine with his dinner.

In the 1830s two of the Alston girls, Emma and Caroline, patiently made up a whole album of their water colours, calling it *Wild Flowers from Odell Wood, Bedfordshire*; this depicted all sorts of delicate wild flowers in the area. The album can be seen in the County Record Office.

OLD WARDEN

This popular village has everything, including a James Bond connection. It is world famous for its Shuttleworth Collection of old planes still flying, it has an Agricultural College, now part of Cranfield University, and its Swiss Gardens rightly feature in top tourist guides. On top of this it is beautiful and historic.

The fairytale charm of Squirrel Cottage, Old Warden

In the early days there was Warden Abbey where monks developed the tasty pear that went to make the Warden Pies that feature in Shakespeare's *The Winter's Tale*. The abbey stood for four centuries until its dissolution in 1537. A stained glass window was given to the parish church by the abbot, Walter de Clifton, in 1381. Nothing remains of Warden Abbey but on the same site is a strange Tudor building, built by the Gostwicks of Willington in the 16th century, that could be mistaken for a folly.

Lands were divided up and Old Warden, meaning 'old watch-hill', went from Sir William Palmer to Samuel Ongley in 1690 and the first mansion was built. It was Lord Ongley, a descendent, who built the picture postcard village we admire today. There are thatched cottages, latticed porches, diamond-shaped leaded lights and dormer windows, decorative pumps and rustic fences, the whole scene created for its picturesque value. There were also stocks for petty nuisances but they must have needed attention for in 1813 one sturdy prisoner broke them open and made off.

Joseph Shuttleworth was the next owner of Old Warden. He came from Lincolnshire, in 1871, where he had been involved in the development of steam traction engines at home and on the Continent. He had the old red brick Ongley mansion demolished and commissioned Henry Clutton to design another one based on Gawthorpe Hall in Lincolnshire. With its lofty clock tower the three-storey Jacobean mansion has become an impressive landmark.

Colonel Frank Shuttleworth, his youngest son, inherited the estate in 1883, married the local vicar's attractive daughter, Dorothy Lang, and they built a reading-room in the village, which later became the village hall. Their son, Richard, was born in 1909, and had the same mechanical flair as his grandfather, eventually starting the Shuttleworth Collection by restoring old cars and aeroplanes. Two of the early machines, a Bleriot and a Deperdussin, had been flown from Bedford polo ground by A. E. Gimmer, an engineer from Ampthill.

Richard went to Sandhurst and obtained a commission in the 16th Hussars. He also flew solo to India in 1933 and, in 1935, won the first British Grand Prix at Donington Park. When the Second World War started he joined the RAF but was tragically killed flying a Fairey Battle on a night exercise. In Richard's memory his mother, Dorothy, established the Shuttleworth Trust, which included the estate, the mansion and the collection. There were enormous difficulties with the development of the college until Mrs Shuttleworth appointed James Bond, not of the 007 fame but an agricultural educationalist. Her vision and generosity rightly earned her the OBE.

PAVENHAM

―――― This is one of the attractive stone-built villages common in north Bedfordshire. It sits by the winding river Ouse which supplied the raw materials needed for the making of rush mats. The House of Commons used mats from Pavenham, made into long lengths suitable for the corridors of power.

Pleasantly dominating the village is St Peter's church, with its tall spire pointing to the heavens. It is packed with quality Jacobean woodwork, brought in by Thomas Abbot Green in 1848 from Pavenham Bury during rebuilding. The big house has now gone but its legacy to the church lingers on.

The church records – as always – have a story to tell. Between 1581 and 1593 there were several children christened whose father is given as Henry Pearcye, a similar name to the noble Percy family, Earls of Northumberland, who consistently used the Christian name Henry. History reveals they had their share of grief: the 6th Earl, in his youth, was engaged to Anne Boleyn and so incurred the suspicion and great displeasure of Henry VIII; the 7th Earl was a Catholic and executed; the 8th was a Protestant and mysteriously killed in the Tower. Lack of males brought the troubled Percy line to an end in 1670.

PERTENHALL

―――― Only a couple of miles from Kimbolton, this small agricultural village, off the beaten track, had two notable men come to stay and leave their mark.

The first was the Reverend John Donne, who shared the same name as another Bedfordshire cleric but was no relation. He was the incumbent when Oliver Cromwell ruled and when there were moves to make him king. Although a Puritan, John Donne was opposed to this on the grounds that parliament, as a body, was better able to rule than a crowned head. He organised the

Bedfordshire petition against the proposal which, with others, may have made a difference. Fortunes change and, at the Restoration, just three years later, John lost his living at Pertenhall and, when he was caught preaching at Keysoe, was sent to prison to await transportation to Barbados. Happily this was not carried out and neither was the Bedford jailer conscientious about keeping him behind bars.

The second man was Thomas Martyn, whose mother was one of the daughters of the prominent King family of Pertenhall. His father, John Martyn FRS, was a professor of botany at Cambridge. Thomas followed in his father's footsteps and also became a Cambridge professor of botany. In 1800 he wrote about Pertenhall, saying that the gentry had deserted the village and esquires were much more common. The present rector had held the living for 46 years and never been absent above a fortnight, except once. In 1798 he said of the harvest that mice were 'remarkably abundant' and were brought into the barns in such great numbers that he was obliged to thresh the corn sooner than he wanted. Earwigs were also plentiful; thousands covered the floor of the carts, all of which was caused by the dryness of the summer, he believed.

By 1804, Thomas, FRS like his father, became the new rector of St Peter's, Pertenhall, and in 1807 he edited Miller's *Gardening Dictionary*.

PODINGTON AND HINWICK

Travelling north from Harrold, along a winding country road, brings us to Hinwick, a hamlet attached to Podington, and there is Hinwick House – a real treasure from the 18th century. Fronted by noble trees and surrounded by green fields, this Queen Anne beauty of 1709 was dedicated by the builder, Richard Orlebar, to his wife, Diana.

Diana brought £6,000 to the marriage, left by her father, Sir Samuel Astry, providing she did not marry without consent. She met this condition by her choice of husband and, by coincidence, the marriage brought her back to the county of her ancestors, who came from Harlington. Portraits show she was a beautiful woman and also very capable. She could, for instance, recall every single item served at any dinner she attended. All culinary matters interested her and one of her fruit cake recipes would probably not

The imposing Hinwick Hall built in 1709 in Queen Anne style

be appropriate today as it needed six pounds of currants and twenty egg yolks to make. Diana also enjoyed hunting which pleased her husband who had a passion for the sport.

Richard Orlebar's parents lived at Harrold Hall and his mother was Jane, née Hatton, a descendant of Sir Christopher Hatton who was Queen Elizabeth I's Chancellor. He obviously got on well with the Queen because when he tried to buy Ely Place in Holborn and the Bishop of Ely refused to sell she wrote on his behalf: 'Proud Prelate, you know what you were before I made you what you are now. If you do not immediately comply with my request, I will unfrock you.' It was the Hattons who owned the site that young Richard Orlebar coveted for his dream house at Hinwick when he was living at Podington Manor and their old manor house is still there, absorbed into the overall plan of his masterpiece. A beautiful clock tower, set amongst attractive Colleyweston slates, dates from this time.

Joining Hinwick is Podington which has an 'olde worlde' charm, partly created by its stone and thatch cottages. Here we have the cricket pavilion which is past its century and has the distinction of having had a middle stump knocked down leaving the bails intact, supported only by the two outer stumps. This incident features on the club's insignia and its place in cricket history is assured. Since there are no public houses in Podington, social amenities are provided by the cricket pavilion and the United Services Club.

At the church a sign reminds us that Podington has won awards in Best Kept Village competitions and nearby, rightly prominent, stands a memorial to precious lives lost in two World Wars. Inside is a dedication on the organ to American airmen who flew their warplanes from Podington airfield between 1942 and 1945. This has since become the Santa Pod Raceway where drag-racing events take place.

POTTON

Merrymaking has played a part in the long history of this pleasant market town, near the Cambridgeshire border. There was even an endowment for 'drinking' after 'beating the bounds' by courtesy of Robert Whyttesyde, at least to the time of the Dissolution. In more modern times we learn of the local lady who lasted five years after her century and claimed she only drank wine and water. Potton was also famous for its 'Apple Florentine' at Christmas which was made up of baked apples with sugar and lemon, covered in pastry and cooked as a pie, then soaked with well-spiced ale served piping hot.

Fire has plagued Potton on three occasions, the worst one in 1783 when many old houses were destroyed. Not surprisingly when three boys came before the magistrates for setting fire to a barrel of tar they were each fined one pound, which was a large sum for a youngster in 1871. Had it been the 18th century a public penance would probably have been imposed as it was when William Thomas called Mary Woodward a whore. He was made to stand in Potton's market square on market day making public acknowledgements, all the morning.

The charter for a market was granted to Potton some time in the 11th century. There were four manors, originally held by Countess Judith, William the Conqueror's niece, who founded Elstow Abbey. The manors, Burdetts, Regis, Rectory and the oddly named Much Manured, became part of the Burgoyne estate of Sutton Park. Potton grew to become a town of some importance with more expansion appearing inevitable, then the railways came and Biggleswade became prominent instead, being on the main line.

Potton was quick off the mark with a local rail link because trains were the hobby and passion of young William Peel, son of the late Sir Robert Peel, the Prime Minister, remembered for giving us 'the bobby on the beat'. In 1852 William had already bought the land between Potton and Sandy but then, as a serving captain in the Royal Navy, left the following year on a frigate bound for the Black Sea and the Crimean War. He joined the naval contingent at the Siege of Sebastopol and in one action picked up a live shell about to go off and threw it back at the Russians. A further action at Inkerman with the Grenadier Guards was also praiseworthy and for his valour he was awarded the Victoria Cross when it was instituted the following year.

Back at Potton he got on with building his railway, buying an engine and rolling stock. The track was laid to Sandy and during excavations in 1856 Roman remains were uncovered including a sword in such good state of preservation that William, being a warrior, kept it for his own use. This was sooner than expected for, before the railway was complete, he was back in action at Lucknow, during the Sepoy Mutiny. He was severely wounded, then caught smallpox and died. Before the bad news reached Potton, Lady Peel, his mother, opened the line and named the engine *Shannon* after his ship. There were huge celebrations with lunch and a pint for 400 people in the Market Place. Slogans praised 'Captain William Peel and Progress'. An old locomotive shed remains from those days and the little engine, with its tall chimney, has been preserved elsewhere.

PULLOXHILL

High on a hill, looking towards the Chiltern Hills beyond Barton-le-Clay, this village with its mix of farms, barns, timber-framed houses and modern dwellings had its church steeple come crashing down in the 17th century, smashing all four bells beyond economic repair. The parishioners struggled on for some years then, in 1740, it was decided the church was so 'ruinous and decayed' that they were putting their lives in danger. Just under £1,100 was needed to rebuild the church and an application was sought to seek donations even outside the parish. The money was raised and, finally, in 1846, Pulloxhill had its new church, six centuries after the dedication of the first St James'.

In the 17th century there might have been a gold-rush in the village when somebody shouted the magic word to describe their discovery. As it happened King Charles II also got to hear of it and his experts seized the mine for the Crown and digging commenced. The top soil was removed then they dug through a layer of clay and iron ore and finally reached the gold-like substance, but it was 'fool's gold'. The field became known as 'Gold Close' and some ancient maps show the 'Gold-mine' that never was.

RAVENSDEN

A name which conjures up the graceful flight of ravens – this village, so conveniently close to Bedford, is where expansion would have been expected. It has certainly been here a long time: the parish church has been restored but Norman traces remain. We also know that Ralph Morin held the manor of 'Mossbury' in the 12th century as we read that he was unwise enough to side with Prince John against his father, Henry II, and had his estates confiscated as a result.

At some time during Ravensden's history a row of thatched cottages was built, part of which seems to have been used as a local court but then become the workhouse, an even more fearful place. Eventually it was made into a pub, one of the smallest anywhere, and was named 'The Case is Altered' which must have given many travellers food for thought. It is now a private dwelling.

Nobody knows how the name came about. There was a theory that when there were roadworks outside, the landlord allowed the navvies to put their drinks 'on the slate'. As work neared completion it was strictly cash only; that is, 'the case was altered'. Another idea was that the 'case' referred to a 'cause' such as that made out for Oliver Cromwell and his republic then altered when Charles II returned.

One of the customers at the pub used to amuse the others by standing on his head balanced on a beer glass. He had ten children and lived in a small thatched cottage next to his cousin who had a fine brood of thirteen. The little cottages were just wattle and daub, built by the fathers of the two men. A huge hedge grew outside and, at Queen Victoria's Jubilee, it was neatly trimmed into the shape of a horse with a jockey patriotically dressed in red, white and blue bunting, perhaps with the help of some of the twenty-three children.

RENHOLD

—— A scattered village with four 'Ends' and one of them, Salph End, only a stone's throw now from Bedford. All Saints, at Church End, is attractively sited and, in these enlightened times, it is hard to imagine that a bath tub was kept in the belfry in 1853 for use when cholera raged.

The glimpse that drivers get of Renhold from the busy A421 is of the parkland belonging to Howbury Hall. Animals graze and sturdy trees thrive in a setting above the river Ouse likely to turn any head. Originally an Elizabethan house stood on the site of Howbury Hall but in 1847 there was a disastrous fire and the owner, Captain Polhill-Turner, called on local architect, James Horsford, to design a replacement. The result was an elegant house in late Georgian style to which the Captain returned from service in the Dragoon Guards, in 1852, accompanied by Emily, his new bride. Three years later he was High Sheriff of Bedfordshire and eventually its Member of Parliament, winning the seat by four votes. Polhill Avenue in Bedford is named after the family who arrived in Renhold in 1781 from Southwark.

It was the Bechers who were at Howbury Hall before then, from 1624. The son, William Becher, was knighted in 1660 and was one of the five justices who presided at the trial of John Bunyan in 1661. He was a kindly man who enjoyed family life, which was fortunate for there was quite a crowd living at Howbury Hall. Firstly, there were the children – he had lost his first wife and was left with two small children, then he had married a widow, who brought her three small children with her, and soon had two more. His two brothers and two sisters also lived with him, and, looking after them all, were ten servants living-in and a coachman. Sir William found it necessary to keep an account and his calculations from 1663 to 1690 have survived, giving an insight into life at the Hall.

Meat for a year was a large bill, just under £100 for a year's supply of beef and other meats but not including fowls and ducks the cook bought at the market. To offset some of the cost he charged his brothers and sisters £18 each for their board. Lady Becher had £40 to spend on sugar, spice, soap and small items sent annually from London plus £100 for her dress allowance. Even the small bills were recorded, like the charity donations – 'one pound for the great fire' and 'ten shillings for the plague' but not 'fiddler at the door' or gifts for his wife like powder-boxes and bouquets, or slipping the children a few shillings when they went to school.

The accounts are in his own meticulous handwriting but the style deteriorates as he records the death of a son – 'seven pounds on funeral rings, five pounds on gloves' but after the grieving we see happiness again like 'my boat to be mended' and 'two hundred rose plants' from Moggerhanger. The account books were fortunately lodged in the County Record Office for all to see.

Renhold lace-makers kept a record of their wedding day by having the large bone taken out of the joint at the reception and a bobbin made from it, suitably engraved, so that whilst busy fingers worked on intricate patterns, thoughts could dwell on the happy occasion.

 ## RIDGMONT

The tragic love story of a beautiful gypsy girl and a vicar will always be told around here because the final scene was played out in this estate village.

It started when Sinetta Cambourne, the daughter of a gypsy horse-dealer in Cambridge, met a graduate from the university who was one of a group of young men hiring horses from her father. Sinetta, an excellent rider herself, also kept the accounts and had dark flowing tresses, a slender figure and an endearing disposition.

Probably many young men fell for Sinetta but the one for her was William Charles Cavendish Bentinck, whose ancestor, the Earl of Portland, had arrived in England with William of Orange. When the couple fell in love William still had three more years of study so it was agreed that Sinetta would stay with a kindly governess who he knew would teach her many of the skills she

Ridgmont

would need, especially as a hostess. After their marriage the
couple moved to Ampthill and William became rector of
Lidlington church. They were happy days but sadly marred by
the loss of their first three children in infancy. This was bad

enough but their fourth, a little boy, held more promise until a nursemaid dropped him on the way to Ampthill church and he died.

Sinetta was grief stricken and could not be consoled. Within ten months the beautiful gypsy girl also died. She was buried at Lidlington churchyard at her own request, having spent many pleasant hours there as the rector's wife.

William was distraught. He left Ampthill in 1850 and became vicar at Ridgmont. Eventually he married again, this time to a Miss Burnaby of Bedford. Their daughter, Nina, in due course married Claude Bowes-Lyon, the 14th Earl of Strathmore, and it is their daughter who is the present Queen Mother.

There are two 'firsts' which can probably be claimed by the village. One was the visit by George Fox, the Quaker leader, to John Crook of Beckerings Park Farm in 1655 which resulted in an open meeting in 1657 when so many came that the proceedings overflowed into the orchard. This was the foundation of the 'Friends Yearly Meetings'. The other 'first' was the Farm School, which opened in 1896, by courtesy of the 11th Duke of Bedford.

RISELEY

——— Ancient cottages and timber-framing remind us of the antiquity of this north Bedfordshire village as does the fine pinnacled church of All Saints with its Saxon-Norman traces. Wresting a living from the heavy soil was always hard and poverty in the past was common – Riseley was one of the villages that joined the Peasants' Revolt of 1381.

From before 1826, when it was first shown on a map, Riseley had a windmill, suitably sited on higher ground just outside the village. It was a post-mill, pivoting on a two foot thick centre post, which meant the whole mill had to be turned into the wind by manpower. Hardy men who worked the mill carved their name on the timbers: there were three Roothams, a Simpson, a Green and Charles Woodward, under whose name was a stern reminder of Judgement Day.

Sacks of corn were brought to the mill by horse and cart and each sack pulled up through a trap-door at the base of the mill by hoist. A story is told that once a sack of corn fell off in the village, unnoticed by the haulier, but discovered by a group of lads. One

Riseley

of them was Joe Smith, a well-built fellow, proud of his strength and physique. The others bet him he could not carry it up to the mill and he took them on for sixpence. He got the sack, which weighed something approaching 200 pounds, on his back, and made his way to the mill, uphill a quarter of a mile away. When he arrived the miller was standing at the top of the steps which led to the first floor. Joe Smith asked him where he wanted it and, for a joke, the miller told him the top floor, expecting him to leave it for the hoist. Without a word the young stalwart climbed up the 22 steps to the first floor then made his way to the top where he dumped the load with such a crash it shook the whole mill. Back in the village he collected his sixpence then spent it, buying the other chaps a drink.

Sadly, the old mill that had withstood so many storms was struck by lightning in 1946 so it was demolished and confined to the pages of village history.

ROXTON

Travelling north-east from Bedford, a right turn off the A421 leads into Roxton village, a place which knew the Danes and the Normans and once paid 33 shillings and 13 score of eels annually for its mill. This was before petite St Mary's church was built which is the last resting place of Roger Hunt, a Speaker of the House of Commons, who died in 1438. There are farm buildings in the village and we hear that Roxton was a pioneering spot for growing Brussels sprouts. Dozens of working horses were kept for ploughing and sometimes horses were caught in the village, having wandered away from lightermen on the river – or more likely their inattentive boys.

Along the High Street is the entrance to Roxton Park and the imposing Georgian mansion, Roxton House. In the park, but opening into the High Street, is an enchanting Congregational church, unique in the county. Built T-shaped, it has an overhanging thatched roof supported by tree trunk columns and it was given Gothic windows which seem perfectly in place. Being a barn originally perhaps explains why it has a backdrop of trees and grazing sheep.

It was converted to a private chapel by Charles Metcalfe in 1808 because he wanted a place of worship closer than St Neots. His sister was married to a nonconformist minister there and another sister also married a minister of the same persuasion so there was a strong independent element in the family.

By 1823 Charles Metcalfe's chapel had become a church with its own minister and both Charles and his son, also Charles, were deacons. At this time the family were holding Fordham Abbey in Cambridgeshire as well as Roxton and, by 1836, Charles Metcalfe senior had twice been Sheriff of the county of Bedford. The family seemed secure and then, in 1850, Charles Metcalfe senior made a serious error of judgement by standing surety for a relative, which proved a disaster. Within a year young Charles Metcalfe left for Guernsey, possibly after a disagreement with his father. Soon afterwards Charles Metcalfe senior resigned as deacon of the church and the minister also left. Roxton House had to be sold, and everything else that could raise money, leaving the Metcalfes in very reduced circumstances but, fortunately, with some loyal friends in high places.

Two of the Metcalfe girls showed great resourcefulness through having to stand on their own feet. They went to France and Germany to improve their education then opened a private school for girls in Hendon which flourished. Charles Metcalfe senior died so their mother went to them, and stayed for 30 years. She died at 85 and was brought back to Roxton, where she had always been highly regarded, to rest in peace with her husband.

SANDY

—— Sandy Beds is an address calculated to cause comment from any traveller intending to stay the night and there must have been a fair few when the Great North Road went right through and travellers left their jarring coach for a comfortable inn.

This town, close to where two rivers converge and the Greensand Ridge begins, was an ideal spot for the Romans and they have left plenty of evidence of their stay to benefit our museums. The soil is perfect for market gardening and it was said, in 1870, that Covent Garden's whole supply of cucumbers came from Sandy. Brussels sprouts were also grown in abundance as transport systems improved.

Poachers could get rich pickings from Sandy Warren with one enterprising man in 1820 doing a deal with a mailcoach guard, James Gittings, to handle all his ill-gotten gains. The Warren had always attracted poachers – in 1792 John Cooper went out looking for them and found a whole gang from Potton who threatened him with violence. Punishment for poaching could be severe but so could non-attendance at church, at one time, and records show local man John Waller 'keeps unlawful rule in his house in service time' and two others were drunk. When Margaret Gibson wanted to marry John Havering, the vicar of Roxton, she first had to get two Justices of the Peace to vouch that she was sober and honest.

The most famous house is Sandy Lodge, the big Victorian building on the outskirts of the town designed by Henry Clutton for Arthur Peel, whose elder and late brother, Sir William, had chosen the site and built his own small house there originally. In 1961 the Royal Society for the Protection of Birds made the house its headquarters and now attracts visitors from all over the world to its nature reserve of over 100 acres.

At the end of the 19th century John Wing had already built Girtford Bridge, something of a landmark and the right distance from London to be the first stop for cycle enthusiasts. Frederick Bidlake became a record breaking cyclist, then President of the Great North Road Cycling Club, and has an appropriate memorial nearby.

 ## SHARNBROOK

This is one of the nice stone villages in the north of the county, handy for the A6 and the river Ouse. Rightly its noble church, dedicated to St Peter, warrants comment: its lofty 14th century spire is an attractive landmark and inside there is a lot of Sharnbrook's history, but something that ought to be mentioned more often is the magnificent lychgate outside. This is one of the best anywhere – made of stone, instead of the usual wood, it is beautifully proportioned and complements St Peter's very well. Additionally, being a proper size, it is in keeping with its real purpose which was a shelter where pall-bearers with the coffin could wait for the vicar to lead them into the church, the name coming from the German word 'leiche' meaning 'corpse'.

Also outside St Peter's, in the graveyard, is a massive mausoleum, quite ornate, and sheltered under an overhanging roof. It belonged to the Magniac family of Colworth House, just one of the many families who have owned the house. It has been built and rebuilt since the 13th century when John Drual started the chain. Right at the beginning of the 18th century Mark Antoine, a London merchant, bought it and built a very impressive house where the old one had stood. Mark had two sons and as John, the eldest, would inherit, he put the younger one, Richard, to an apprenticeship as a linen draper. John died prematurely so Richard inherited anyway and never needed his drapery skills. The last owner was Lord Melchett and then, in 1947, the house was acquired by Unilever.

 ## SHARPENHOE

—— Sharpenhoe Clappers must rank amongst the finest views in Bedfordshire. Whatever the weather the sight always impresses. No wonder the rolling hills at the edge of the Chilterns were Bunyan's 'Delectable Mountains' in *The Pilgrim's Progress*.

It is unusual that in such a small hamlet, being just a part of the village of Streatley, two such accomplished men as Edmund Wingate and Thomas Norton should have a connection.

Edmund, the son of Roger Wingate of Sharpenhoe, was the renowned mathematician who went to Paris after graduating and ended up teaching English to Henrietta Maria, the future queen of Charles I. The other figure of distinction, Thomas Norton, was born in Sharpenhoe in 1532 but then raised in London where his father prospered. Thomas was educated at Cambridge and became a successful lawyer, working with Archbishop Thomas Cranmer, also from Cambridge, who was father of the English prayerbook and had the ear of Henry VIII. Later Thomas married the Archbishop's daughter but then Queen Mary came to the throne and his father-in-law was burned at the stake. This influenced him in later years when policies were reversed and his severity earned him his nickname 'Rackmaster General'. Prior to becoming a Member of Parliament, Thomas had absorbed himself in the arts and, in collaboration with Sir Thomas Sackville, he wrote a play called *Gorboduc*, an experimental work which was performed in London for Queen Elizabeth I in 1561. The result was profound and paved the way for the works of Marlowe, Ben Jonson and Shakespeare himself.

Thomas wrote other pieces over the years but made his money through his legal practice. Sometime just after 1578, he bought Shapenhoe Manor and saw out his few remaining years.

SHEFFORD

Not many years ago, people saw more of Shefford than they wanted as they queued to get through before the bypass eased the bottleneck. Earlier, any complaints on market day that traders' stalls in the High Street caused a restriction to large vehicles could have resulted in the 13th century charter being produced which shows that only the width of two carts needed to be made available.

Shefford's centre is attractive; the High Street leads into Northbridge and Southbridge Streets and some nice old buildings stand there, like the half-timbered house with overhanging upper floor, making an archway below. Across the road a plaque on the front of a house shows where Robert Bloomfield, the pastoral poet, lived and where he died in 1823. His most famous work was *The Farmer's Boy*, which was based on his own experience at his uncle's farm. He was too puny for that job and went to London at 14 to learn shoe-making from his brother, turning up in boots so big that wedges were placed behind his heels to keep them on. He is buried at nearby Campton because that was where the graveyard for the area was.

St Michael's church dominates Shefford's High Street

Shefford's two bridges, giving us Northbridge Street and Southbridge Street, show where the rivers Hit and Flitt pass through the town and in 1822 the river to Langford was canalised by the Ivel Navigation so that barges could reach the town. At that time a windmill stood at the water's edge which worked up until about 1880. The bare shell has stood there every since, plainly seen from the B658, needing only imagination to have the sails turning in the wind again. Across the town Roman remains were discovered in 1826 which are some of the most important ever found in the county. The best piece is a beautiful blue glass jug, skilfully ribbed and intact, which can be seen in the Museum of Archaeology, Downing Street, Cambridge.

Before 1962 trains went through Shefford, crossing the High Street by a bridge. Knocking it down opened up the view and was an improvement but the old bridge was so sturdily built by the Victorians that it took twice the time expected to demolish it. Also in the High Street is the parish church of St Michael which was rebuilt in 1822 but has a stocky tower from the 14th century. James Haddow earned a shilling a week at the church for winding up the clock, general cleaning and, on Sundays, prodding those in the congregation who had dozed off during the sermon.

 ## SHILLINGTON

When the tower of the parish church came crashing down in 1701 the bells that had rung out for victory over the Armada came rolling down the hill and, it is said, landed in a stream.

They certainly fell from a great height for Shillington's All Saints' church crowns a hill 568 feet high and dominates the village – and the half a dozen 'Ends' that belong to it. It would be half a century before the bells were returned and the tower rebuilt.

The climb up Church Street, past all sorts of houses and cottages tucked into their space on the hill, is well worth the effort if only to see the views across an agricultural landscape with the rolling Chiltern Hills as a backdrop. No wonder there is a sign at the bottom of the hill telling us it is a scenic route.

Opposite the church gates are old school buildings where a vicarage once stood and, alongside, a pathway called The Twitchell once provided another route for children going to

Apsley End, Shillington

school. Attendance suffered because many children went to so-called plait schools in the 19th century where they could earn money making straw plait for the hat trade. One caring vicar inadvertently improved school attendance by giving the hungry children a bowl of porridge before lessons.

Rural life was hard and poverty rarely a stranger. Laws were harsh too as a plot of land named 'Gallows Field' indicates. There were no 'Scales of Justice' emblazoned on the local Court House, instead sets of manacles decorated an outside wall, perhaps as a deterrent. In the early 1830s, fearful that the Shillington men might riot like neighbouring villagers, a load of truncheons for Special Constables was delivered to the church – never to be used and never collected.

Buried treasure was found locally in the 19th century, in the form of fossilised dung from prehistoric creatures. These phosphatic nodules, or coprolites, were badly needed by the fertiliser industry and there were plenty in the village just a few feet down. Anybody who could use a spade got to work and others found employment in the washing sheds. The village thrived and soon 1,400 people were engaged in this new occupation. So many newcomers arrived that the school population trebled.

Coprolite-digging did not last as foreign imports at the turn of the century provided a cheaper alternative, but it had come at an opportune time and is part of village history.

SILSOE

——— A bypass gave this attractive village peace at last from the A6 traffic, still within earshot, and now allows visitors to linger long enough to see the variety of ancient cottages, some timber-framed, and one of the few lock-ups left in the county.

The shapely church of St James was only built in the 19th century; the one that stood there before had a central tower which had a new spire added by Thomas, 2nd Earl de Grey, but collapsed under the weight. The building of the new one was supervised by the Earl, who became the first president of the British Institute of Architects.

Many local people were estate workers for the de Grey family of Wrest Park, and they were the lucky ones. For others poverty was a constant fear and a workhouse was erected to deal with the unfortunate. The one at Silsoe had a manager on a salary of £95, who seems to have earned every penny. It was agreed that nobody with smallpox, or other diseases including the 'itch', should be admitted until cured. In contrast a Wrest Park servant, with the colourful name of Tryphosa Box, was comfortably settled in a Silsoe cottage on her retirement.

The history of the village is entwined with Wrest Park and the de Greys who first appeared in Bedfordshire in the 13th century and stayed for six centuries.

After a chequered history, Wrest Park itself was purchased for the nation in 1947 and leased to the National Institute of Agricultural Engineers. This became the Silsoe Research Institute of today which, together with English Heritage, ensures that the house and gardens receive the attention such a county treasure warrants.

SOUTHILL

──── When the celebrated diarist, John Byng, described Bedfordshire in 1794 as 'this garden of a county' he could have been thinking of the countryside around Southill which he loved. This attractive mid-Bedfordshire village was made into a parish by adding it to Broom and Stanford.

It was popular with Dr Johnson and his companion James Boswell who used to visit Squire Dilly, as he was known, at Yew Tree Farm and Dr Johnson, who was a welcome guest almost

The Glebe House, Southill

everywhere, stated that at Southill he found 'an abundance of excellent fare and hearty welcome'. As a party piece, he used to recite his reply to Lord Chesterfield who belatedly offered him patronage: 'Is not a patron one who looks with unconcern on a man struggling for life in the water and, when he has reached the ground, encumbers him with help?'

Many of the attractive dwellings in Southill were either built or restored by Samuel Whitbread, who bought the estate in 1795 from George Byng, the 4th Viscount Torrington, an admiral who had served his country well and made a fortune in prize money. His hapless son, John Byng, was not so lucky as an admiral: he became the scapegoat – although his expedition was ill equipped and undermanned – when Britain lost Minorca to the French in 1756.

Admiral Byng was found guilty of neglect of duty and shot at Portsmouth in 1757 on the quarterdeck of HMS *Monarque*. His body was brought back to Southill and a plaque over his tomb in All Saints' church, close to his father's, does not mince words. The first line reads 'To the perpetual disgrace of Public Justice', and this was the general opinion.

STAGSDEN

This village west of Bedford and close to the A422 belongs to another time. Thatched cottages still grace the streets, just waiting to be photographed, and St Leonard's church, with its short spire sitting on top of a stocky tower, has been a witness to village happenings since the 13th century.

Many people worked on the land and there must have been some substantial holdings in 1803, when we were expecting an invasion, for when emergency transport returns were made Stagsden could supply twelve waggons and five carts for the army.

Bad roads and unsprung vehicles made travelling extremely uncomfortable in times past, but they could be dangerous as well. Dorothy Kins, a local girl, was crippled in 1707 when the coach to London overturned, causing her to lose her job as housekeeper to Sir Anthony Chester. Loss of employment could mean the workhouse, which was dreaded. Thomas Peck of Stagsden was in the workhouse but ran away. He was gone for two days then returned, probably through hunger. When refused supper until certified by the overseer, he struck the master's wife, Sarah Davis, with a tin vessel.

In 1965 a Bird Garden was opened which had exotic birds of all kinds on display. Many species were bred there and people travelled for miles to see them. Unfortunately thieves came as well so some of the beautiful birds were lost and sadly this worthwhile venture was discontinued but, for a lot of people, Stagsden was synonymous with birds.

STANBRIDGE

A common surname, Stanbridge is believed to get its name from 'stone-bridge', perhaps from a bridge of stone across a brook south of the village. In those days it was a hamlet of Leighton Buzzard and at one time had an aptly described chapel of rest to save the long trek to a place of worship. Later the church of St John the Baptist was built, which stands dominantly by The Green.

The church is built of ironstone, with Totternhoe limestone being used in the chancel and south aisle. This attractive limestone was a favourite material for churches throughout the county. Strangely enough, even with such a plentiful supply of

St John's church by the green in Stanbridge

stone close by, the half-timbered building method was preferred for houses in the village. From this spot in Stanbridge there is a fine outlook across the downs and, in the other direction, the sails of a grand windmill once turned. Fortunately the shell remains, giving meaning to the name Mill Lane. Rather unlike Station Road which no longer leads to a railway and only old maps show there was ever a railway line.

Stanbridge had to struggle to get a school in the 19th century. They formed themselves into a group with Eggington and Tilsworth and met at the Five Bells Inn to organise the joint venture. Finding suitable sites that the owners would sell proved the biggest problem and it was 1881 before schools were built, eleven years after the Education Act.

STEPPINGLEY

Money talks and when Walter de Steppingley slipped the Sheriff of the county, or his deputy, 20 shillings he was spared the honour of a knighthood, with its royal obligations, and allowed to peacefully farm his land at Steppingley.

The village sits on a double bend which slows motorists down on the Flitwick to Woburn road and gives them a glimpse of the

Steppingley

ancient French Horn pub, and its near neighbour the parish church of St Lawrence together with a battlemented former school building. Both were built by Henry Clutton, architect for the Duke of Bedford, who built churches in other estate villages in the 19th century.

St Lawrence's predecessor was thought by some to be the smallest church in the county, with a tower scarcely the height of a haystack. When visited by the archdeacon in 1823 and 1826 he pointed out structural defects and warned against water gathering at the base of the walls. Nothing was done and, in 1858, much of the church fell down. The new church was completed within two years, the rector contributing towards the chancel. It was followed half a century later by a thorough restoration at the Duke's expense which included work on the foundation of the chancel. This uncovered 500 silver coins, mostly English but a few Irish and foreign examples amongst them.

STEVINGTON

Tourists come to this village and rightly for it has a fully restored windmill from the late 18th century which is worth travelling to see. This one is a post-mill, built around a large centre post, and the miller had to turn the whole body, above the round house, to bring the sails into the wind. A lot of work was done locally on the mill in 1921 and then it continued working until 1936. It was in 1951 that it was acquired by the County Council.

The village centrepiece is an ancient stone cross and St Mary's church, which has traces of Saxon material in its tower, is tucked away down Church End, with the river beyond. Pilgrims flocked here in the Middle Ages to get water from the Holy Well believed to possess curative powers. From the early 16th century they would have seen St Mary's unusual bench-ends. They show ordinary situations like a student at his desk and someone else drinking from a bowl.

About 1140, Baldwin of Ardres, a small town near Calais, took possession of Stevington church and 140 acres of land, for the benefit of Harrold Priory. Over a century later a dispute raged between the prioress and the vicar which could only be settled by the ecclesiastical court. At least the vicar got rights to the game but the prioress retained the rest.

The ancient stone cross stands in the centre of Stevington

One of the rules, to try and keep law and order in the 13th century, was that perpetrators of crime should be detained by the community, or the village could be fined. Stevington fell foul of this law for when Gilbert, a carter, shot John le Messager in the stomach with an arrow so that he 'died at once' in front of the whole village, nobody tried to stop him and he escaped. Nobody intervened either to stop William Soames, a local farmer, from being assaulted by his own workmen in 1826 in spite of the loud threats being made at the time. It happened at 'Harvest Home' when he had given his men supper. Unfortunately he also gave them far too much beer which was unwise for someone as unpopular as him.

STOTFOLD

Handy for both Baldock and Letchworth, and enjoying town status, Stotfold spreads itself ever closer to the Hertfordshire border. Livestock travelling to London along the Great North Road would be penned up overnight and many couples stopped off to get married. Mills were built close to the river Ivel and Malthouse Lane reminds us there was a brewery at one time. Coprolite, the droppings from prehistoric animals, was dug here as well as further west (see Shillington), and it was also a market gardening centre.

St Mary's is the parish church and has its share of antiquity. A new vicar turned up in December 1754, the Reverend Samuel Roe, and stayed for 26 years. He was married to a Bishop Stortford girl, Ellen Roberts, and they raised a family of four boys and four girls. Sadly one girl died at 18 but all the other children were blessed with longevity, two reaching 90, like their mother.

Reverend Roe was vehemently opposed to a new preaching method particularly practised by the Quakers and Methodists, labelled 'Enthusiasm', which accurately described what it was. It was condemned for its power to persuade, inspire and enthuse the listener. The Reverend believed that only those with apostolical authority and licence should preach. He went so far as to suggest that there should be a law to cut out the tongues of the offenders.

In spite of his extremist views he seems to have been happy with his lot. He died at 68 and was buried at St Mary's, joined 32 years later by his wife. It seems the whole family stayed in this border area as there are several graves in the churchyard. The youngest son, Henricus Octavus, who lived to be 92, was a successful solicitor practising in Baldock. He was a major benefactor of Stotfold and when he died he left over £12,000 to form the Roe Charities.

STREATLEY

——— One end of this village sits near the top of Barton cutting overlooking the hamlet of Sharpenhoe and the other butts up to Luton down the busy A6.

There, for 50 years, stood St Margaret's Home for Elderly Men which was also a haven for those 'gentlemen of the road' tramping the highways on their perpetual journeys. Now, in the same general area, stands the modern Pasque Hospice, a tribute to popular endeavour.

The village church, also called St Margaret's, has witnessed quite a few changes over the centuries. Once almost in ruins it now stands whole again mainly through the generosity of an

American, Edward Harkness, who gave £2 million in 1930 to form the Pilgrim Trust which funded restoration projects across the country. It was carried out under the watchful eye and expertise of Professor Albert Richardson of Ampthill.

Cleaning the walls brought to light a picture of a lady with a wheel whose identity remains a mystery though St Catherine has been suggested. Another mystery is the font which is at least a century older than the 14th century church. Old records tell us that before 1559 St Margaret's was white inside but it was not liked by one Robert Norton so he paid 20 shillings to have it repainted, 'with texts of scriptures in English if it, by the law of England, may be suffered.'

The Norton family were prominent in Streatley for ages but none became famous like their kinsmen Thomas of Sharpenhoe, though Richard Norton would have been something of a celebrity for starting a village school in 1686 at his own expense. Years later the records tell us about another school opening: ' I Eleanor Howgill opened Streatley Board School this morning June 4th 1883.' It closed in September 1982, just nine months short of its century – it was the end of an era.

☙ STUDHAM

——— Our most southerly village sits on the Downs in a green and pleasant spot looking towards Buckinghamshire and Hertfordshire. The 13th century church of St Mary is tucked away down Church Road, and from the same era we know there was already a windmill in Studham because a widow was claiming one third share.

In 1598 William Bemond got into trouble with the law over his non-attendance at church and whatever sentence it was he received it seemed to work for the priest states, 'I do now find him very comfortable in that he voluntarily came unto me to have it effected'. Only a few years later, at the archdeacon's court, Amy Chauncellor of Studham stood accused of being a 'Brownist'. She was not alone in her belief in the Independent Church that the Reverend Robert Brown of Norwich is usually credited with founding, for by 1633 Archbishop Laud found Bedfordshire to be 'the most tainted of any part of the diocese'.

Studham was involved in the straw plaiting industry right from

Studham

the start. The nimble fingers of women and children brought much needed funds into poor households, so when legislation favoured the wool trade Studham folk joined in the protest of 1689.

In 1707 the Reverend George Burghope died in the village, but he was not forgotten completely for money he left supplied bread to the poor of Studham every year on the anniversary of his death.

SUNDON

Sundon Park Road is a well-known thoroughfare in north Luton running through a large residential area of the town and leading eventually to the south Bedfordshire villages of Lower and Upper Sundon, which are separated by a steep hill.

The parish church of St Mary is in Lower Sundon and the road bends around it. It dates from the 14th century and when it was built stone seats were fixed along the wall for those who could not stand too long, presumably when the church was full. It was a question of the 'weakest going to the wall'. Remembered in the church are Lord and Lady Sundon, who had an impressive mansion nearby and entertained many distinguished guests in the 18th century.

Lady Sundon was born Charlotte Dyve, granddaughter of Sir Lewis Dyve of Bromham. She married a William Clayton and, probably, would have remained unknown except she was liked by the influential Duchess of Marlborough, Sarah Churchill. This led to her appointment as Gentlewoman of the Bedchamber to Princess Caroline of Ansbach, the future queen of George II. The two became close and Charlotte was able to influence the German princess and, through her, the Prince of Wales. When the princess became Queen Caroline people seeking advantages at court did so through Charlotte. They then showed their appreciation by gifts of expensive jewellery, following a not unusual practice though some people said by wearing them she was advertising her position of influence.

At this time, George II appointed her husband William to high office at the Treasury and later he was created Lord Sundon. His marriage to Charlotte was a happy one; they remained childless but frequently had nephews and nieces staying at Sundon. Letters have survived and in one Voltaire was so impressed by the kindness shown to him in London by Lady Sundon that he wished 'for the honour of Versailles and the improvement of virtue and letters we could have here some ladies like you'.

Lady Sundon died in 1742 followed by a saddened husband ten years later. The estate was divided up, with a share going to his niece Elizabeth Cole whose husband William was Sheriff of the county. In this capacity he invited John Wesley to preach the assize sermon at Bedford and then to visit the Coles at the Sundon mansion. Wesley made the journey on horseback in 1758 but the road to the village had become a mire and he was forced through ploughed fields which were not much better. In due course the estate was sold to the Page-Turners of Battlesden and they demolished the old mansion.

SUTTON

—— Driving through Sutton's ford past the 14th century packhorse bridge is a real pleasure, all the time the water is low, and the scene here has been reproduced countless times by generations of artists and photographers. The bridge is unique in the county and so is the sacred barrel organ, in All Saints' church, which dates from 1820.

By 1823 the vicar, Edward Drax Free, was being accused by the churchwardens of drunkeness, stealing lead off the church roof, keeping livestock in the graveyard, fighting in the church and fathering three illegitimate children. Being able to prove all this was a different matter it seems for Edward was still vicar seven years later, though on his way out. An earlier vicar of All Saints was Edward Stillingfleet, 1658 to 1664, and he was so remarkably handsome they called him the 'Beauty of Holiness'. He moved on when other opportunities beckoned and eventually became Bishop of Worcester.

TEMPSFORD

With two rivers converging and as there was once also a ford, it is not surprising early settlers came here. Unfortunately for the Saxon population the Danes came too, using long boats on the river, and Tempsford became the scene of violent struggles. In the 14th century parish church of St Peter, separated from the village by the A1, there is a stained glass window commemorating the great victory over the Danes by Alfred's son Edward, in AD 912.

During World War II, Tempsford became the centre for Special Operations, formed to fight a secret war in occupied Europe. The idea of agents working with resistance groups to sabotage supply and communication lines was conceived by Hugh Dalton, the Minister of Economic Warfare. Two special duty squadrons were based at Tempsford, 138 and 161, who were later joined by airmen of the Polish Flight. Their planes ranged from tiny Lysanders, which could put down and pick up agents from the smallest field, to the twin-engined Lockheed Hudson which was also extremely versatile.

In one daring operation, two of these larger American machines flew to Dijon in France, picked up 20 people and returned unscathed. The future President of France, Vincent Auriol, was one of those rescued. Pilots were very vulnerable, not only to enemy action but also to the hazards of improvised airstrips, as Flight Lieutenant Guy Lockhart found out, to his cost, in August 1942. He had already completed seven missions to France, picking up agents in a Lysander, but on the eighth the plane went into a ditch and was wrecked. He set it on fire and then headed for Gibraltar and, two weeks later, was back in Tempsford.

Before the war, Guy Lockhart had been a pilot officer but got dismissed for reckless flying over an airfield. When the war came he re-enlisted as a sergeant-pilot and flew fighters before the Tempsford transfer. Now it was time to move on again; he had one more successful mission then switched to flying with a pathfinder squadron of Lancasters and later became a Wing Commander with the DSO, DFC and Croix de Guerre. He was killed in action over Germany in 1944.

Wartime exploits from Tempsford stir the imagination and many books have been written on the Special Operations Executive activities, carrying out their task of 'setting Europe ablaze' as Churchill described it. Royal acknowledgement was given to this 'fourth arm' when the King and Queen visited Tempsford in 1943. All that is left from those days is the barn where the agents were fitted out for their dangerous missions.

THURLEIGH

Up until 1941 this small village just north of Bedford was, like many others, not well known. It sits on a plateau, where a castle once stood, and people got their living from the land. It was part of the Wrest estate in the 13th century and, by the 16th century, the manor with 400 acres was let to Thomas Caldwell for £100 a year. St Peter's with its cruciform shape and stocky tower is from Norman times. Here an unusual carving was made, in stone above the door, showing Adam and Eve together with a serpent entwined round a tree depicting their temptation. Down Mill Hill the sails of a working windmill turned until 1917 and without them it looks rather like a lighthouse.

From 1942 Thurleigh became very well known, having given its name to the huge airfield on its doorstep. From here American B17 bombers of 306 squadron, nicknamed 'Reich Wreckers', took off on their air offensive, earning citations and sadly suffering losses. It seemed that no sooner had they transferred to Germany after the war than work started on the Royal Aeronautical Establishment, a research and development extension of the Farnborough complex, which changed the landscape.

Not surprisingly, when the Roskill Commission was looking

for a suitable site for London's third airport in the late 1960s Thurleigh was a strong contender, for one thing it already had a first class runway and the very best equipment. Thurleigh was regularly in the news as protests increased until Stanstead was selected. Those days have all gone but the runway remains as a reminder of more active times.

TINGRITH

Tucked away in the heart of Bedfordshire this village ranks amongst the smallest but only in size for it has more than its share of stories to tell. One would be the amazing record of the Reverend Edward Tanqueray and his son Trueman who served as vicars from 1787 to 1899, watching over their flock for 112 years. During their long vigil we lost America but won at Trafalgar and Waterloo; still in their era came Queen Victoria who even with her 60 glorious years only outlasted the younger Tanqueray by two years. Father and son were buried in the parish church and their names on the list of incumbents are a permanent record of their extraordinary service.

Tingrith church is dedicated to St Nicholas and was rebuilt in the 1500s with attractive battlements even on the stair-turret and, just outside the shapely porch, a beautifully carved Victorian tomb in the mould of a wedding cake. Here lies Robert Trevor, at one time the lord of the manor. The stained glass windows were mostly crafted by William Bolton in the 19th century who had previously lived in America and visitors to New York can see more examples of his beautiful work at St Ann's Centre in Brooklyn. He returned to this country to study theology at Cambridge, was later ordained and never used his remarkable gift again.

Maintaining our historical village treasures like St Nicholas' church has always been a problem and records show that maintenance of the bell clappers was once so overdue that Jim Smart, the sexton, was convinced he could be hit on the head by one at any time with dire consequences. Being smart, not only by name, he put health and safety first by leading the ropes out of the danger area, and chiming the changes from a nearby staircase. Unfortunately by the time the bell clappers were renovated a deep groove had been cut into the arch-stone of the

Tanqueray House, Tingrith

doorway leaving an unsightly reminder. One bell had a special chime and was nicknamed the 'Potato Bell' – it was rung at the end of the service to tell the servants at the Manor it was time to put the potatoes on.

The village had its ups and downs over the years. In spite of its isolation the plague still got through in 1665 when burials increased including three from one family. It is believed that the infection was spread from Woburn where it was particularly severe. Swine fever struck between 1878 and 1882 and wasted a thousand pigs before leaving the village in peace.

TODDINGTON

Just a few miles north of Dunstable, on high ground in pleasant countryside, the ancient village of Toddington endures its changing fortunes. Long gone are the days when it was a thriving market town prominent in the straw plait and other local trades. These past prosperous times are reflected in some of the fine buildings around the attractive green.

The right to hold a market was granted in 1218 by Henry III at the same time as St George's church was being completed. Quite a few changes have taken place over the past centuries like the addition of a clerestory in the 15th century and the extensive restorations in the 19th century.

The church has a parvise, described in the church guide as originally being a chapel and priest's living quarters. It is believed to be the only one of its kind in the country. The tower of the church is central and is surmounted by an oak cross dating from the 17th century. It was the Peyvre family who built the church originally and they also erected a palace so magnificent as to be 'admired by all its beholders'. Nothing remains of this building but the Peyvres are remembered in the church.

As well as notable times of prosperity and prominence, Toddington also had hard times, such as in 1362 when too few men were left alive to manage the land after the plague had done its deadly work. The manor was also without a 'lord' for some years when Thomas Wentworth, the Earl of Cleveland went to the Tower for six years for his Royalist activities. He was exiled in 1648 and died abroad, leaving his wife Philadelphia and small daughter Henriette to return to Toddington with his father in 1660, at the restoration of Charles II.

Philadelphia now held the manor on behalf of young Henriette and under her management stability returned. By the time she was 17 Henriette had been presented at court and noticed by the Earl of Thanet, who Philadelphia thought would make a favourable husband. Henriette also met the princesses Mary and

Anne, both future queens, and the handsome, dashing, but married, Duke of Monmouth.

They fell in love and when Henriette was brought home to Toddington he followed her and stayed at the manor. The proposed marriage plans had to be abandoned as her love affair with the Duke flourished. When Charles II was searching for his errant son in connection with the Rye House plot, which he thought involved him, Monmouth was with Henriette at Toddington Manor, lying very low.

The manor house is approached by a long drive, which runs from a gatehouse on the road towards Woburn just at the edge of the village. Although still a large house, it does not compare in size to the mansion which was there before. The hearth tax returns of 1671 list the manor house then as having 45 hearths, so by all accounts a sizeable property.

The builder of the great house was Sir Henry Cheyney who was connected to the Wentworth family, and one of the rooms he named 'Royal' for this was where he received his knighthood in his own house from Queen Elizabeth I whom he had entertained.

In the extensive grounds that surround the house there is water and shady trees. It was said that for many years a tree in the park still bore Henriette's initials carved into its bark by Monmouth. The young Duke enjoyed many happy days at Toddington with Henriette as notes found in his pocket after his arrest for treason indicated. The eve of his execution was spent with several bishops trying hard to make him declare that his love for Henriette had been a sin, but Monmouth refused; and kept on refusing even when he was denied the Last Sacrament. He persisted all the way to the block in his belief that 'that which hath passed between us was very honest and innocent in the eyes of God'. With the love of her life dead, Henriette pined her life away at Toddington Manor and within a year she was laid to rest with her ancestors, in the Wentworth Chapel of St George's church.

In due course the Earl of Stratford took over the manor and he demolished over three-quarters of the building to make it a suitable house for his steward to live in. All manner of beautiful things were disposed of including several fine wood-carvings, one apparently going to the Old White Horse at Hockliffe. It seems the villagers were incensed by the demolition, even though the building had fallen into a state of disrepair. For years there was a poem that passed on the sad tale:

If Lord Stratford had never been born
Or in his cradle had died
the Old Manor House would have always stood
And many a tree beside.

TOTTERNHOE

When the Saxons came to this spot beneath the shadow of the Chilterns and found the hill spur they built a look-out tower on top which gives the village its name. The Normans came next and constructed the biggest motte and bailey castle in the county, leaving us the earthworks off Castle Hill Road to visit as Totternhoe Knolls.

There are three 'Ends' to the village, Church End, Middle End and Lower End, and originally local landowners were responsible for keeping the road repaired. This was not easy on a well-used road and they were frequently in trouble, particularly from one Dunstable Justice, Marshe Dickenson, who harassed them through 1760 with the threat of fines.

Although many people lived off the land, Totternhoe also had the quarry where its famous stone came from. Men worked underground carrying a light, in tunnels that were often wet, hacking away at the stone with pickaxes for others to haul to the entrance for the hewers – just as they had always done. When the owner died in 1762, the business was put up for sale and, in praise of the quality of the stone, it was said several thousands of loads had gone to Woburn Abbey and to other noblemen's seats all around. It could also have added St Albans Abbey, Windsor Castle and scores of churches throughout the region.

In this period, when George III was on the throne, a Totternhoe heiress married the Member of Parliament for Aylesbury, John Wilkes, and must have been devastated when he published a paper libelling the King, which got him and his friends thrown into prison under a general warrant. She must have been equally relieved when he proved the arrest unlawful, the libel parliamentary privilege, and extracted a thousand pounds in damages from the other side.

Totternhoe's Doolittle Mill, so named because water power from its stream was so poor it 'did little', shares its name with another at Ampthill but at Totternhoe they did something about their problem by building an adjoining windmill to help it along. Unfortunately it was put out of action in 1880 during a severe gale but remains an example of ingenuity.

TURVEY

This attractive stone village was made that way by design but its position helped, being on the river's edge, looking across an ancient bridge to neighbouring Buckinghamshire. Just here stands the statue of Jonah, erected in 1844, and his local 'wife' from more modern times, curiously with a man's head complete with beard and hat.

Anglers come to Turvey and just before the bridge there is the Three Fishes with another inn, the Three Cranes, nearer the centre. Here, leading into All Saints' church, stands a handsome lychgate, restored by a grieving father, Charles T. Lindsell, in loving memory of his only daughter and three grandchildren, lost at sea in 1925.

The Mordaunts became the dominant family in Turvey; they had been in the village before William Mordaunt took over the manor in 1310 when he was county coroner. Later Mordaunts held high office, in the county and nationally, with Sir John Mordaunt being raised to the peerage in 1532. Being Roman Catholic later became a disadvantage and, as a child, the 5th Lord Mordaunt was removed from his mother to make certain she could not influence him. He was created Earl of Peterborough in 1628 but the title became extinct in 1786 and the manor was bought by Charles Higgins Esquire from Weston Underwood who was a 'London Merchant'.

This was a godsend in the making for Turvey. He bought Turvey Abbey along the Bedford road, which was never an abbey just a private house built on church grounds but, oddly enough, now houses an order of nuns. Charles Higgins remained unmarried and his estate was divided between a nephew, John Higgins, who received the Abbey, and a kinsman of the same name who built an impressive mansion in a park, Turvey House.

Sons born to these men became the benefactors of Turvey, Charles Longuet Higgins of the Abbey and T. C. Higgins of Turvey House. They rebuilt Turvey in the golden stone of today, with cottages having four rooms, an outhouse and good garden,

The sumptuous chancel of Turvey church

for 15 pence per week rent as described in 1865. This Charles Higgins studied law and medicine and the community benefited from his knowledge. He maintained more than Turvey's share of the bridge and engaged Sir Gilbert Scott to sympathetically restore All Saints', taking great care of the fine Mordaunt monuments there. Afterwards he donated an organ which he played on Sundays.

Charles Higgins was well loved by Turvey folk but not by the local hunt for he shot foxes on his estate yet, whenever they were being chased, the foxes would disappear into his garden. It was discovered that they had found sanctuary on the roof of an outbuilding by clambering up the ivy-covered walls. Another fox crossed the river at full flood at Turvey and the riders following ended up unseated and struggling in the water. Tragically, a Silsoe man, John Edwards, was killed in the melee.

T. C. Higgins shared Charles' humanitarian attitude which became evident during his time as chairman of the quarter sessions. He was also a romantic and when he first fell in love with his future wife, Charlotte Price, the chairman's seat remained empty because he had completely forgotten the meeting.

WESTONING

——— The last village before the M1 on the busy A5120 southwards from Bedford, Westoning made headlines in 1976 when, before dawn, a fuel tanker crashed and set houses ablaze at the crossroads. Fortunately there were no fatalities and all has been rebuilt, with traffic lights and calming measures, but memories remain. A distinctive feature at the crossroads is the Chequers, fortunately unscathed, which is an attractive example of an 18th century inn. Church Road starts here and leads to the church and the manor.

The village was originally called Weston; the 'ing' coming from Sir William Inge, a Chief Justice for Edward II. He had held the manor for some years before 1299, for by then almost all Westoning belonged to him, and in 1303 he was granted a charter for a market and annual fair. He also rebuilt the parish church, which benefited the nuns of Elstow.

Sir William got involved, on the 19th June 1312, in a very controversial matter for, on that day, the barons dragged Piers Gaveston to the block and summarily beheaded him. The King was outraged and devastated at the execution of the handsome Frenchman, his dear friend and close companion. Afterwards the Canon of Bridlington said the executioners had first sought the advice of Sir William Inge who had not found their intentions illegal.

Life was often hard in villages, getting a living off the land, and Friendly Societies sprang up in the 19th century, to arrange mutual support for workers. Westoning's group met at the Chequers and the rules were very clear. Their funds were kept in a box with three locks and each member contributed. During sickness some money would be available and, if necessary, an apothecary provided. There was also a death benefit of five pounds. Any member drinking too much, swearing in the meeting or trying to raise a bet would be fined twopence.

WHIPSNADE

Whipsnade is world famous now that we know the best way to see wild animals is in their more natural state but the few people who lived here in 1931 must have wondered what effect the zoo would have on their lives.

The old village only had a population of 36 in 1600 but they were well established for at St Mary Magdalene's church the tower was being built on an older church with locally made bricks. The vicar, Nathaniel Hogan, was seen to be 'fit to officiate' in 1646. The Vaux family were prominent, with John on the parliamentary committee. This beautiful part of Bedfordshire, the largest chalk downland in the county, has stunning views from its lofty situation and the 'bags' that could be obtained from a day's shooting of pigeons and game birds were well known.

Putting a zoo in a country park was the brilliant idea of Sir Peter Chalmers Mitchell of the Zoological Society and in 1927 420 acres were purchased from the Ashridge Estate Trustees, and more bought later. As the intended park would entail changing footpaths and removing other ancient rights, parliament had to come up with the Zoological Society of London Act 1928 before the 6½ mile fence could be erected.

Everything was ready by 1931 and special trains ran from Euston for several days, transporting the overcrowded animals from Regent's Park Zoo to their spacious Bedfordshire home. It must have been quite a sight seeing elephants, camels, giraffes and buffalo tramping along country roads. The opening date was 22nd May 1931 when over 2,000 people attended a private viewing. At the first public holiday 26,000 turned up, adults paying one shilling and children sixpence, and the first half million was reached in 1932. The experiment was a huge success and Whipsnade Wild Animal Park has achieved a whole string of 'firsts' – and is likely to continue to do so.

To complete the picture we have the great White Lion to see, some 160 yards across, and the Tree Cathedral, not far from the village green, which is a 20 acre area of many different trees, planted by Edmund Blyth in memory of fallen friends from the Great War. Whipsnade is a valued local amenity, as well as a tourist attraction.

WILDEN

Just north east of Bedford, Wilden is mentioned in the Domesday Book and means 'willow valley'. It was always an agricultural area, surrounded by farms, as well as various 'ends' and people made their own enjoyment. As early as 1610 it was recorded that the young men of Wilden played football, but it would have been forbidden when services were taking place at St Nicholas' church.

One young man who kicked over the traces and became 'troublesome' to his father was John Feazey. As a result he was promptly dispatched to Australia which was not uncommon in the 19th century. It had the desired effect for, reflecting on his waywardness, he agreed that sending troublesome sons across the sea was the best thing a father could do as 'that will bring them to their thoughts very soon'. His biggest regret at being moved from Wilden was over his lost love, a Miss Dean.

To return to earlier days, the rector of St Nicholas' church in 1604 was Francis Dillingham MA who was chosen in that year to be one of the translators producing the authorised version of the Holy Bible. It is possible that he used it at Wilden before its publication in 1611. He never overlooked the needs of the parish and tried to improve the lot of the poor.

One of Wilden's early benefactors was Thomas Peate who left money to provide for a school master but only on condition that he was to be dismissed if he should 'live disorderly or be contentious'.

Lionsfield Farm House, Wilden, built late 16th century

WILLINGTON

When marauding Danes got to Bedford to wreak their customary havoc on the population, whilst looting the churches of anything valuable, they came via Willington because that was as far as they could get by boat. Centuries later Ouse navigation stopped at Great Barford for many years, due in part to the Civil War, so Willington lost out again.

Although only 4 miles from Bedford, along the busy A603 to Sandy, it would be easy to miss the turn into the village but fortunately a 'Village Loop' sign and a picture of a dovecote guide the way. The 'loop' is made up of Station Road and Balls

St Lawrence's church in Willington

Lane connected by Church Road and attractive dwellings abound from half-timbered thatched cottages to more substantial houses and a sturdy pub, the Crown.

An event which had far-reaching implications for the village occurred in 1380 when Robert Gostwick got the job as bailiff for the Mowbrays who held the single manor. By his efforts his descendants rose to be gentry, no mean achievement, and by about 1485 there emerged the most dynamic one of them all, John Gostwick, who acquired power and great wealth. By 1529 he had bought Willington from the Duke of Norfolk and was lord of the manor.

John was a great opportunist who had managed to keep his head when all about him were losing theirs, for Henry VIII was on the throne. His chance had come through service to Cardinal Wolsey who took John into his household and involved him in the pageantry and popular entertainment of the day. Costumes played an important part in Tudor revels and John started importing colourful hats and caps from the Continent. Contacts in the textile industry saw him admitted to the Mercers Company and he accompanied the King and Cardinal Wolsey, with their vast retinue, to Calais for fourteen days of festivities. It was such a magnificent affair it was called the 'Field of Cloth of Gold'. John's helmet and tabard from this great event were eventually placed in Willington church.

When Wolsey died John lost no time in making contact with his talented assistant, Thomas Cromwell. He forwarded a letter saying, 'I send you by the bearer a calf and two dozen pigeons, the best novelties I can send you at this time'. The gesture was not wasted, and, when Cromwell found favour with Henry VIII, he did not forget John Gostwick. He was appointed Treasurer and Receiver General of First Fruits and Tithes, which were benefits once given to Rome but now the property of the Crown.

Being in an ideal position to acquire monastic properties made John very rich and he built up a huge estate in Bedfordshire. He enlarged his Willington holding by using stone from Newnham Priory to build the superb dovecote we see today, that can house well over 1,000 birds, and the adjacent two-storey stable block in a similar style. Both buildings are community treasures and popular tourist attractions. He also rebuilt St Lawrence's church, which makes a noble landmark at the far end of Church Road. John's fine manor house stood nearby; it was not very large, having only 18 hearths, but lacked nothing by way of comfort. In 1539 Thomas Cromwell stayed there for a few days whilst Henry VIII was at Ampthill Castle, the two men enjoying friendship through mutual interest.

Only a year later Cromwell, now Earl of Essex, lost out to rivals and was executed, which cast a shadow over John, being an associate and friend. Very shrewdly, John 'found' monies that Cromwell had apparently missed and Henry VIII was so pleased he rewarded him with a knighthood. Furthermore, in October 1541, he stayed at Willington with his newly made knight, thus giving Sir John's manor royal approval.

The Gostwick family lasted in Willington for nearly two more centuries but never produced another character of Sir John's calibre. The final scene in the Gostwick saga was played out by Sir William who became Sheriff of Bedford in 1679 but had his eye on a political career. In the general election of 1698 he won the seat through buying votes, for example by picking up bar bills in numerous Bedford inns. He remained a Member of Parliament for the next 15 years, using the same improper tactics on seven occasions, and it ruined him. By 1713, at the end of his career, he owed over £26,000 and was reduced to accepting aid from the

Whig party until his death in 1720.

It seems that his grandson and heir could not turn the business around with such a huge burden of debt and, in 1731, he left the impoverished estate for good. What had been built by endeavour had been lost on a whim. By 1774, Willington and the old Gostwick estate lands in Cople, Ravensden, Renhold and Goldington belonged to the Duke of Bedford. The former Gostwick manor house apparently suffered a fire and was then restored by the Duke but with little of the original building remaining.

WILSTEAD

Bypassed by the A6 south of Bedford, this village provides a link to the A600 road to Shefford and is a convenience, just as it was in 1814 when John Morris, an Ampthill brewer, drove his heavy waggons through the village to avoid a tollgate charge. Ironically he damaged the road so badly in the process he had to make amends.

Wilstead was not a wealthy parish and when the church tower fell down in 1742 one Saturday night, fortunately after evening service, there was no money to repair it properly. It was well over a century before the tower was restored and a new chancel built, giving All Saints' the church we see today. Resting in peace here is William Morgan, who was Prime Minister of South Australia in 1877 and died visiting Wilstead in 1883. He had left the village many years before as a poor emigrant but found gold and amassed a fortune.

There were many men emigrating to the colonies from Wilstead; 34 went in the mid 19th century and one, named Rogers, sent home £20 for his wife and four children to follow. She applied to the parish for the balance required and, although they could not help her themselves, they did give her leave to approach the better off herself for donations. They approved of her excellent character so it is likely this family was reunited.

The Armstrongs of Wilstead were staunch Methodists, in fact the first chapel in the village was built by William Armstrong in 1808. Being farmers, tilling the land was their headache as current ploughs were very inefficient. One of the Armstrongs designed a plough which he got the local blacksmith to make up.

It was so good that fellow Methodist James Howard of the Britannia Iron Works in Bedford mass produced it as the 'champion plough of England'.

WOBURN

—— So easy to take for granted, world famous Woburn Abbey and the Safari Park rightly attract thousands to our county and the historical estate village is part of all this. Graced by many Georgian houses, red brick and bay fronted from an age of elegance, Woburn speaks of days past when coaches rattled over cobblestoned streets at this important crossroads.

It had town status then, hence the town hall facing Park Street, and close by a bull-ring was used to tether beasts en route to market. Somewhere here a Queen Eleanor's cross was erected after the sad funeral procession had passed through in 1290, but no trace remains. Cistercian monks were at the abbey then and remained until their abbot spoke publicly against Henry VIII marrying Ann Boleyn and was hanged from an oak in the park. After the King's death Edward VI gave the abbey and manor to John Russell who became the first Earl of Bedford by 1550. William, the 5th Earl, became the first Duke of Bedford after his son and heir had been needlessly executed in 1683 by Charles II.

Woburn suffered some disastrous fires, accidentally started, except for the one by Royalist troops at the start of the Civil War when 27 houses were destroyed. Another one in 1724 accounted for 39 more but these were fortunately rebuilt by the 4th Duke. The achievements of the many Dukes that followed are well documented and make interesting reading. An outstanding contribution was made by the 9th Duke who believed that the minds of children were affected by their environment and made sure that, in estate villages, good housing and schools were available. When the authorities took responsibility for education after the Act of 1870, they received 24 schools from the Woburn Estate for a nominal rent of ten shillings each and, even then, the estate picked up the maintenance bill. Many years later the 11th Duke summed up by saying that the Bedford system of land management has not been carried on with gain as the principal object.

A more obvious contribution was made by the 8th Duke when

The High Street, Woburn

he called in Henry Clutton in 1865 to design a new parish church in Park Street. Made of Bath stone this gem of a building beautifies the entrance to Woburn Park and is a tribute to its provider. For capturing the imagination, the Flying Duchess is top of the list. This remarkable woman had multiple interests in addition to aviation and excelled at them all. She became a fully qualified theatre sister and designed a cottage hospital which became Marylands College in due course. Sadly the duchess's aircraft crashed into the sea in 1937 and only some wreckage was recovered. A stained glass window in the church is dedicated to her memory and her love of wildlife is indicated by birds in flight.

A Woburn man who caught wild birds was 'Arthur' who lived, until 1918, in an estate cottage which cost him sixpence a week. He had 13 children and needed his wits about him to feed them. Knowing cage birds were all the rage, he trapped sparrows, dipped them in yellow dye and sold them as canaries to Woburn visitors. Fortunately, as it turned out, he became so flea ridden from the birds that they reduced the rent to sixpence a fortnight because nobody wanted to collect it.

WOOTTON

Lying just off the A421 to Kempston in sight of Stewartby's tall chimneys, this old village can reflect that it was making bricks before its new neighbour was ever conceived. Then the place was called 'Wootton Pillinge'.

Like many villages, Wootton is large in area, encouraging development, but it has a compact and historical part centred on St Mary's church and the manor house. It was to the original manor house that George Monoux arrived in 1514 direct from London. He had prospered as a draper's merchant, had recently been Lord Mayor, and now wanted a country seat.

The family stayed and by 1635 Sir Humphrey Monoux was the Lord of the Manor and Sheriff of the county. Charles I was reigning and had just imposed ship tax, causing a national outcry. Bedfordshire was assessed at £3,000 and Humphrey, an ardent Royalist, managed to collect nearly all of it when many areas raised hardly any. When Civil War came, Humphrey managed to be excused from billeting troops at his large manor house even though other people were not so lucky.

Loyalty to the Crown was absolute in the Monoux family and when the Duke of Monmouth landed in 1685, to try and seize the throne, young lieutenant Philip Monoux dashed off to Somerset to take part but was killed before the battle even started. A memorial tablet in the church commemorates his sacrifice.

Another settler in Wootton was Thomas Russell, a maker of watches and clocks, who arrived about 1697 soon after his marriage. Two sons were born, Thomas and William, and both went into their father's business as well as his sideline which was casting church bells at a foundry he had started. Between them they made over 70 bells, many ringing the changes in churches around the county, including Wootton's own St Mary's.

The boys were not interested in continuing the bell-casting after their father died in 1744. Then two decades later another clock-maker came to Wootton who, coincidentally was also into bell-casting. His name was William Emerton and by 1768 he was producing quality bells from the Wootton foundry. St John's at Bedford ordered five bells but they could only pay for one and William was stuck with the other four. He managed to sell one to Eversholt church before he died, and this, it is believed, was the last bell ever cast in Bedfordshire.

INDEX